BRIGHOUSE AND CLIFTON REMEMBERED

Marjorie Shooter

Bloomington, IN  Milton Keynes, UK

AuthorHouse™
1663 Liberty Drive, Suite 200
Bloomington, IN 47403
www.authorhouse.com
Phone: 1-800-839-8640

AuthorHouse™ UK Ltd.
500 Avebury Boulevard
Central Milton Keynes, MK9 2BE
www.authorhouse.co.uk
Phone: 08001974150

First published by AuthorHouse 5/16/2006

ISBN: 1-4259-2874-9 (sc)

Printed in the United States of America
Bloomington, Indiana

This book is printed on acid-free paper.

The author

Acknowledgments

I would like to thank my niece Julie and my great niece Kathryn for their help with the typing and organisation of the text, my nieces Shirley, Mavis and Julie for the loan of photographs, Geoff and my great nephew James for assistance with computerising the images, my daughter-in-law Bronwen and her great nephew Thomas for reading and offering advice about the text, my great nephew Ben for help with scanning and web pages, David for suggesting that I could write a book and my husband for his patience and support throughout the writing period.

Marjorie Shooter 09.01.06

CONTENTS

CHAPTER 1.

'17 violins, 30 pairs of shoes and an exploding oven'.

I was born on July 27th 1919 at Clifton, a hilltop village just a mile from the little town of Brighouse in West Yorkshire. Mrs Auty was the Clifton Midwife at that time and before she handed me to Mom she carefully smoothed my head, and said, "There that's a good shape". She then said I was a "farl tarl" meaning ugly. This was in case the devil came to take me away with him. I was christened Marjorie.

Marjorie, born 27/7/1919
A larger version of this photograph was kept on top of the
piano in the family home and all visitors were told that

Clifton was, and still is, just a small village, but there are many more houses now than when I was born. Originally there were three pubs (although one has closed down) a Church and a Methodist Chapel, a Post Office, a Co-op store and three sweet shops, two of which were made from the front rooms of houses. The other sweet shop was at the top of our terrace, in Kiln Fold. Maybe originally that too had been just a house, but somehow it always looked more like a shop. All three had a bell on the door so that the lady could hear if a customer came in. They would be busy doing their housework in the back, but break off immediately to come and serve.

Most of the houses in Clifton were very old and one farmhouse even goes back to Saxon days. The Romans had built a road going from Clifton to Brighouse through a part of the river that was easy enough to make a ford for them to cross. I often wondered if our back street was part of this Roman road, but the teacher thought not, she thought it came a little lower than our house in Forrester's Terrace, and came through the field below.

Our house was new when Grandad, Mr Irvine Baldwin, came to live in it with his wife Eliza and children Annie, Lucy, Elizabeth, Albert, Joe, Frank and one more whose name I forget. His wife died in her fifties, but Grandad stayed there the rest of his life, living with my Mom and Dad and eventually with us, his five granddaughters. When it became possible Dad bought the house from the Forrester's Friends' Society.

139 Clifton Common (the family home on Forrester's Terrace) around the beginning of the 20th century.

It was a two bed roomed house with a front room and kitchen, quite lofty rooms and spacious bedrooms, but no bathroom. Because we were such a big family we even put a bed on the landing at one time and had two double beds in the front bedroom along with a large wardrobe, dressing table, wash hand stand and huge chest of drawers. There was still enough room to get between the double beds, to make them in comfort.

Whereas there were two windows in the front bedroom, the back bedroom had only one. It had room for the double bed and a large cot, a dressing table and a curtain across a recess where clothes were hung. There was also a large migration chest behind the curtain and a large chest of drawers fitted into the other recess. We had wallpaper that was covered with rosebuds, which I tried to count once when I slept in the back bedroom. The big cot was next to the bed. It was a yellowy coloured wood and I can remember the taste of it as I once sucked some knobs that were on the corner of the rails. When my youngest sister, Isobel, was born she stayed sleeping in the cot until she was two or three years old. It was a big cot, almost as long as a bed.

The kitchen was square and had an iron range along one wall, which had to be black-leaded and the edges rubbed with emery paper to buff them up. A side pan had water in it, always hot, and on the other side of the fire was the coal oven where everything was cooked and baked. When it was a day when the oven wouldn't draw it meant it needed cleaning and then it was very exciting. Mom lit a firework, a little demon cracker and dropped it in a special compartment with a metal shutter. I always ran outside at this stage and listened for the bang. Soot would all shower down into the metal compartment. Mom held a shovel and poked a long rod rake into the soot, pulling it onto the shovel. This cleaned it out and the oven would then draw and get to the correct heat for baking all the lovely bread and tea cakes, twists and loaves and cobs which we ate every week.

The dough for the bread was kneaded in a large baking bowl, yellow on the inside and a terracotta colour on the outside. A cloth covered it while it waited to rise. It was put on the hearth for the warm fire to work on the yeast in the dough. We had a large baking board, a long rolling pin and lots of bread tins - loaf tins which were greased before filling part way with dough. Baking day was a lovely day. The smell of the new bread in the warm kitchen was a delight. The kitchen had a high shelf running the full length, full of shoes: thirty pairs of shoes maybe, all in a row. Eight people used a lot of shoes! Wellingtons were kept behind the cellar door.

Washing and ironing was the week's biggest job and I still think it is even today when all we do is pop the clothes into a washer and drier and then iron. In those days we had to use a posser, rubbing board and mangle. We had to have a lady to help because of the large quantity of washing. We always had a clean dress on every day. Mom didn't lower her standards as some did when they had a large family, and Dad did two jobs. He always said, "They didn't ask to be born". We were all looked after like only ones and we also learned to look after each other. We stayed very close always.

We had jobs allotted to us, as we got older. First the cellar steps to wash, and when you made a good job of them you could move onto the outside toilet. We had to use wool cloth for the stone floor and cotton cloth and scrubbing brush for the wooden seat. When that was all satisfactory a younger sister did it and I moved onto the front flags, which had to be ruddled. [1] As I was doing it I used to draw faces upside down for my younger sisters to laugh at from the room window. White edges were put on the five steps up to the front door and the two steps down to the pavement, with a whitening agent called donkey stone.

The house is still in our family to this day. The road camber was altered and the pavement raised and now it's just one little step to the pavement.

When I was young Grandad did the front garden and grew prize auriculars, which he always called 'recklesses'. He kept a five-shilling piece to measure the flowers, and if they covered it he knew he'd win. He gave cuttings to many people but they never produced these big flowers when they left Grandad's garden. He would never let us gather a flower even when the teacher asked us all to

---

[1] Ruddled – scrubbed with a yellow stone found in quarrying.

bring one. He said they lasted far longer to leave them where they were. We always had to go round to Mrs Oldfield's for one of hers. She always said "yes".

The front room housed Grandad's shut-up bed and the piano, as well as the settee and chairs. Grandad had a cratch chair, which he placed by the window, near the fire. The fireplace had tiles, blue and white pictures and the words, 'The mill will never grind with the water that is past', printed on them.

Grandad Irvine Baldwin, in a cratch chair, in the front room.

We always had to have a piano and of course all the violins were stored all over the house. We had 17 violins. They were on top of drawers and everywhere you could think of, in every available corner. Dad was a musician and one of his jobs was teaching the violin, another was playing in the evenings for silent movies or other occasions where a string group was needed. If a poor family could not afford an instrument Dad would always lend them one. People gave him violins too sometimes.

Dad, Frank Sutcliffe, playing his violin in the back garden c.1964.

One violin always stayed in a corner just by the door leading into the kitchen. It stood on slippery polished lino, which surrounded the carpet. If anyone happened to run past and brushed against the fiddle box, it fell down in the corner and then when Dad came to use it all the strings would be down and out of tune and he knew it had fallen and asked who had been rushing around knocking violin cases over!

Once a burglar broke into a large house further down Clifton Common and stole a violin and then left it on a wall all night. During the night there was a heavy shower of rain and the violin got soaked; it wasn't in a case. Someone found it on the wall next morning and took it to Dad. He spent a day on repairing it and then played it when he'd finished. It had a lovely tone. He thought it looked like a home made violin, but it was so beautiful that he went down to the police station to report how it had been given to him and that he suspected it had been stolen. The police asked how much it was worth and Dad explained that it would be hard to say. The police said Dad had to keep it safe and they would be in touch. Well eventually it dried out, but when Dad played it again it sounded really terrible; the very worst sound that ever came out of a violin. Seemingly it had to be all wet to make a good tone and it was no good at all! What a disappointment.

My parents were both musicians, they first met when they both had lessons from a Mr Boothroyd of Brighouse. There was an orchestra called 'The Permanent Orchestra', all male members. My Mom, Annie Baldwin, wanted to join so asked the conductor, Mr Hanson Hayley, if she could be a member. He said she could, if she took her sister Lucy to sit by her, seeing they were all men. After a few weeks she asked the conductor if she could sit by Frank Sutcliffe, my Dad. She then told her sister she didn't need her to come sit by her anymore, she'd be alright next to Frank Sutcliffe.

We heard this story often when we were children and used to tell Mom she was 'forward', asking to sit by Frank Sutcliffe. Of course he soon carried her violin case, and eventually they married and had five daughters. I was next to the eldest.

Her brother, Albert Baldwin, who was a wood carver, made my mum's first violin for her. He was quite well known for his work and carved some beautiful screens, reredoses, in churches. The violin was a little bigger than usual and Dad helped with the tuning. Mom was quite a good violinist and had a lovely bowing action. Later when we had our own family orchestra Mom played and never did any practising; she hadn't time to practise, but she could just pick it up and play as though she'd only played yesterday, and it could have been six months since she made music.

Music was in all of us children; we could all sing in tune from birth. As we lay in the pram we sang the note of Blakeborough's buzzer [2] every day. Dad would say, "She'll be a singer!"

---

[2] The hooter at the local factory

CHAPTER 2

Five Sisters, Mom, Dad and Grandad.

When I was two years and three months, my sister Kath (Kathleen) was born. I was taken to stay at Grandma Sutcliffe's for two weeks. Grandma spent the time teaching me to dress and undress myself, doing up buttons and tying a bow. I remember folding my clothes as I took them off, putting them in a pile, and then turning it over so that they were put on in the right order. I wore lots of layers of clothes; a vest, then a liberty bodice with a lot of buttons, a warm petticoat and a fancy cotton petticoat with an embroidered hem and scallop edge, then my dress, and of course knickers, socks and shoes. It took the whole two weeks to train me. The warm petticoat fastened with a button at the back of my neck, and that was very hard to fasten, also the drawstring in the fancy petticoat had to be tied in a bow and that was hard too.

Grandma was Dad's stepmother and had never had children. She realised Mom would be busy looking after the new baby, so she made me independent. When I went back home Mom said I never wanted her to do anything for me ever again. Dad realised I must have had my nose pushed out, so he nursed me when Mom was busy with Kath. I became "Dad's girl".

Altogether we had eight in our house: Grandad Baldwin, who lived with us 25 years, Mom, Dad and, eventually, five daughters. I wrote a poem [3] once about the family, which was all very true. It's lovely to be one of a large, loving family, you always feel secure and that nothing can ever harm you. It gave me confidence to face life's difficulties. The family was always there and always loyal. Sadly I ended up with only one child myself, due to an illness I had as a child damaging my heart and making childbirth a strain on it, but that comes in a later chapter!

For us children spending money day was Friday when we got a penny. Grandad used to say, "Give it to me and I'll keep it for you, better than taking it to the shop." Kath once did give Grandad her penny and he wouldn't give it back! It took ages to get it; I never gave him mine!

---

[3] See chapter 16

Dorothy Mary, author's eldest sister c.1919

My eldest sister was called Dot (Dorothy Mary). She was five years older than me and Mom always told me about anything that Dot had done wrong, so that I wouldn't do it ever. Like the time Dot wanted a penny to buy a lucky turnover and Mom said no it's not spending money day until Friday. A lucky turnover was made of hard icing sugar. It had a heart shaped case and was pink and white. The base contained a ring in a piece of tissue paper. The lid was sealed on and it was all made of icing sugar.

When Mom was out of the room Dot found her purse and took out a penny, went up to the sweet shop and bought the lucky turnover. She brought it back home to eat and of course Mom said,

"Where did you get the penny?"

Dot said, "Your purse."

Mom threw the lucky turnover on the fire. We thought it a disaster to burn a lucky turnover, but of course we didn't ever do the same thing ourselves.

There were quite a variety of sweets to be bought for a penny. 'Tobacco', which was a cocoa flavoured sweet wrapped in a tube of thick paper, everlasting strips of liquorice (Spanish), Spanish spoons, sherbet dabs, kali, aniseed balls, mint balls, love hearts, liquorice and violet pastilles, gums, bulls eyes, five boys chocolate bars, lemon drops, Yorkshire mixtures, Liquorice torpedoes, toffee apples, acid drops, Easter eggs, little biscuits with icing sugar on, penny cornets, pomfret cakes, toffees, wine gums, fruit pastilles, boiled sweets, popcorn, liquorice root (horrible!) and dolly mixtures.

Some of these sweets I never bought, as I liked pink coloured boiled sweets. We weren't allowed to buy Kali because it coloured our fingers and Mom said, "Think what it would do to your stomach." My favourites were the five boys chocolate bars, everlasting strips of liquorice (Spanish), Spanish spoons, sherbet dabs, love hearts, aniseed balls and toffee. When I grew up Mars bars were invented and I loved them: two pence each, or two for three pence at Mr Who are You's.

Mrs Greenwood, at the bottom house in Forrester's terrace, used to make slabs of homemade toffee. It was truly delicious and far nicer than any bought sweets.

When I was very young all the people who sold pots and pans, paraffin, coal, vegetables, yeast, fish, firewood, teacakes, oat cake and potted meat in brown pot dishes, all came round in a pony and trap, or horse and cart. We bought our groceries from the Co-op. Everyone had a Co-op number and received a check for the amount. These small checks were kept on a wire hook and when Bonus Day came round they were all added up to find the total of how much had been spent. It was then worked out how much Divi we would expect to receive. I think it was about two shillings and sixpence in the pound. Grandad used to add up the checks. He could do that very well. We then all received a penny. A Divi penny was wonderful, as was the gas penny when the man came round and emptied the meters. These were extra to the Friday penny spending money. 24 aniseed balls for one-penny, a sherbet dab, or an everlasting strip, tobacco in a paper tube, gob stoppers, sherbet fountain, lemon drops, pear drops, Turners toffee, five boys chocolate. The little shop just above the terrace of houses, used railway timetables made up into cones to hold the sweets. Not many proper white sweet bags were used. The timetables were free.

Grandad was a very good weather forecaster. No woman in the terrace would dream of washing heavy woollen blankets if Mr Baldwin forecast rain. They called out over the hedge "What's it going to do today Mr Baldwin?" and Grandad always seemed to be right. He forecast the weather after he studied his mug of coffee. Mom had to pour the water on without stirring, and it was the formation of the bubbles that said if the weather would be fine, or wet. Grandad said it was the action of the atmosphere on the coffee. If it was to rain I think the bubbles were at the sides of the mug. Grandad didn't get the pronunciation correct, and always said the "Tompashear" for the atmosphere. Many old people had similar faults. One old lady I knew called Mrs Bottomley, said "Troppoline" for Tarpaulin, and "Euporium" for the new Co-op emporium. They left school at eight years old. Mrs Bottomley went into service at a farm, and wasn't given enough food, so if a hen laid away she found the eggs and ate them raw! Grandad went down the pit.

Leaving school at eight years old to work down a pit must have had a traumatic effect on a boy so young. His nose had black spots on it which was coal embedded in his pores. He once killed a weasel, which he thought was going to attack Kath in the pram. Poor weasel, it would have been more scared of us I shouldn't wonder. Grandad played draughts and dominoes, but couldn't read. We have wondered since if he could have been dyslexic. He was good at maths and certainly could grow auriculars. He used to say to us "Never say No, when you mean Yes".

After Kath came Nora; she was about five years younger then me. My sister Nora once gave us a real scare. Grandad was sitting by the fireside in our front room, and Nora was playing and she fell backwards on to the fire. My Dad was just coming downstairs and saw what had happened. Grandad was unable to get up and pick her up and Dad jumped down five stairs and leaped across the room and picked her out of the fire. Her hair was singed, and she was very shocked, but otherwise unhurt. Grandad was full of apologies, but he was very old by this time and couldn't get up quickly enough.

I had most in common with Kath, there being only two years difference in us. Nora was five years younger, and until we were both chosen for a concert to be given on Christmas day at Prize Giving at Sunday School I didn't feel as close. Nora would be three years old, nearly four, when she had to be a will o' the wisp and I had to be a fairy. I had to take Nora to rehearsals and we seemed to bond. She had to carry a torch and kept lighting it all the time and the battery ran out at the show and Nora kept stopping and blowing it to make it light up as she had seen done on bonfire night with touch band.

The youngest of us was Isobel. I was nine when she was born and our family was complete. I thought it was wonderful to have a new baby. I was thrilled to bits, and loved nursing her. She never cried because I would say "I'll pick her up" straight away. Mom even thought Isobel's lungs might not develop because when I wasn't there to nurse her, the next door lady used to say "pass her over, I'll see to her", and she went over the privet hedge.

I remember taking Isobel out in the pram, and once, just as we crossed Saville Lane, the pram was at an angle and a strong wind blew and tipped it over, and Isobel fell out. I quickly put her back in and didn't say what had happened for quite a few years. Once we were talking together about when Isobel was little and I admitted tipping her out of the pram and Kath said the same thing had happened to Isobel at the same place when Kath was in charge of the pram. Neither of us had told Mom!

I also remembered nursing Isobel and sitting on a low stool when suddenly she flung herself backwards. She didn't bump her head and I pulled her back by her long nightdress. Kath said the same thing had happened when she nursed Isobel after her bath. It was amazing that Isobel grew up into a normal little girl after all these near disasters!

Mom was born in December 1892; she is the little girl on the right, on the back row of this school photo.

Mom, Annie Baldwin, back row, last on the right c.1900.

In those days the girls all wore pinafores over their dresses and the boys had knee breeches and stiff collars. Sometimes Mom would describe the dresses she wore. One was pale grey alpaca with lead trimming. The lead was points on the end of the belt. I could never imagine it being smart; lead seemed so dull and grey, but Mom insisted it was very smart. They wore elaborately trimmed large hats and dresses with frills round the hem. A dressmaker made the dresses and often Mom and her sister Lucy were dressed alike. They wore boots.

Annie and Lucy Baldwin as girls)

Mom only worked for six months after leaving school. She worked in a number of mills, leaving for more money each time. If they were paying sixpence a week more at another mill she went there. After six months she stayed at home to look after her dad and brothers and sisters, as her mother had died. The rest of her life was spent caring for her own large family and her father, who lived another 25 years after his wife died. Once or twice he tried to find another wife, but Mom told him she would always look after him, when she could see that he wasn't finding anybody suitable. She kept her promise up to the end.

We didn't have the doctor much when we were all small. We had to eat good food, which was always tasty, and Mom knew all about vitamins and proteins and gave us a lecture, why we had to eat up our veg. She was ahead of her time really. When I got to Grammar School and was learning these things I was the only one in the class who knew anything about it. The teacher asked how I knew and I said, "My Mom tells us so that we know why we should eat things". She said, "I think you must have a very modern Mum".

Children died young in those days. One grave in the churchyard was a little girl. I used to go with my friend Polly and regularly tend this grave. We saw that it always had a few flowers. We took one flower from other graves and kept a jam jar of water clean and fresh on this special little girl's grave. There was no headstone, but we decided it was a little girl's grave.

Mom really was very, very good, looking after five of us, and Dad, and Grandad. She never raised her voice. I hadn't ever thought about that, but when she died a neighbour, who had two boys, said to me, she envied my mother because she never ever raised her voice to us, and this neighbour used to shout at her two sons all the time.

Mom couldn't ride a bike, and we tried to teach her and ran holding the saddle, but she never really managed it. We all rode bikes from an early age. We stood up on the pedals when we couldn't reach the seat. Once my first bike had a skirt guard, which needed renewing. The skirt guard was put there to prevent the long skirt of the lady riding the bike becoming tangled in the spokes of the wheel. I went to the Co-op and asked the manager for some sugar band. Sugar was weighed out into blue bags and tied up with blue and white sugar band, a very strong string. It was then threaded through holes along the edge of the mudguard down to the hub of the wheel.

The Co-op manager often weighed me on his big scales that weighed out flour and Indian corn in a back room. Treacle was in a round metal drum in a corner with a tap at the bottom, and the jar was held under the tap. When the man added up the groceries on the counter that we'd bought he said the price three times and then moved onto the next item. It seemed he was being very quick adding it all up, but he wasn't really. Boys came for flour and brought two cloths, a white one and a check one to carry the flour. They carried it on their heads. People wouldn't have bought bread in those days, unless they had teacakes occasionally. Our Mom was a good baker and we had home baked bread always. My mother-in-law was equally as good, and excelled at oven bottom cake. It was superb.

We had visitors only occasionally when we were at home. I remember an aunt and uncle with their three children once coming for tea. We had to lay the table in the room, as the kitchen table was only big enough for seven of us. The large oak table in the room had two leaves. An iron handle fitted into a hole underneath the top at one end. It was turned and opened a big gap, which was then filled up with the two leaves. A complicated mechanism underneath worked this wonderful contraption.

I was playing at Polar Bears with cousin Vera. Somehow her head went up between this middle extension arrangement, as Mom was opening the table. It caught Vera's head and held it like a vice. A twist in the wrong direction would have cracked her skull, maybe killing her. Dad rushed in and he turned the handle the right way to open underneath. Auntie Gertie and Uncle Albert put their hats and coats on and took their three children home. They couldn't stay for tea, as all of us were so upset. It was terrifying.

Vera, left, and Hilda Baldwin

Dad went to night school after he was married. He didn't go to Grammar School; maybe it hadn't opened in Dad's time. Dad and another boy called Tart were taught Latin at school, just the two of them. This Mr Tart's daughter became my friend at Grammar School and she told me about the Latin. So Dad must have been a clever scholar. He was always a reader and loved Dickens. Our house was full of books. He encouraged us to read and was very keen that we should have a good education, so we all had to do our very best and try hard. We all five went to Grammar School and knew it was a big sacrifice for them to keep us at school until some were 17 and 18. I left at 16 and got a job straight away starting immediately after the summer term in 1930.

Dad always had two jobs when there was work. He had a light job, in the joinery during the day, then dashed home and had a good wash. He spent a long time always on his hands, scrubbing them and drying them carefully. Rheumatism in his hands would have been a disaster. He wore evening dress, and had to walk to Clifton station to catch the train to Halifax. His clothes were laid out on the bed, and he only had a limited time in the house. It was turned midnight when he got back. Up again at 6am. He did two jobs always, and had pupils at weekends.

When he started work as a boy, his father worked at the same cotton-spinning mill. If Dad's machine broke down he just fetched his father to mend it. His father realised that Dad should be learning how to mend his own machine, so he waited till Dad had a big breakdown then he walked out of the mill, telling him he was leaving. Then he went to get another job, doing the same work, at another mill and leaving Dad to mend his own machine. It took him three weeks. It was all laid out on the floor and by the end of three weeks Dad understood how every part worked.

The machines were called 'jinneys' and they were huge, long machines for spinning cotton, moving backwards and forwards all the time. When an end of cotton broke it had to be knotted by a special knot. He told me that the men who understood the machinery ran the machines, which ran smoothly, and didn't break the cotton. Some ran about fastening up the ends all day long, working very hard. Dad said the glass eye could get sharp and cut the cotton, so if one end kept breaking he would run his finger round the glass eyelet to feel if there was a sharp bit that was causing the breakages. Once mended it ran smoothly again.

When I didn't like my homework Dad would say, "I am just needing a little cop lapper". And I would say, "Oh let me, let me!" Then he would become very serious and say, "No! There's none of you will ever work in the mill." He was very determined and that's why we all had to aim for the Grammar School. Quite a number of boys and girls passed the county minor, but their parents didn't let them go. They had to work and bring in a wage. Girls especially weren't often sent to Grammar School as parents took the attitude they'd soon get married anyway, so there was not the same incentive. It was also felt that boys were cleverer and girls would be better to learn homemaking skills.

CHAPTER 3

Primary School

Clifton School was quite small, having a classroom for infants, with another small room to the side, which was used to store stock, and three other rooms for children to be taught up to the age of 14 years. The infants would be five years old and the next classroom held children of six, seven and eight; even nine years old if they hadn't done very well with the year's work. They stayed until they had improved. The next room was Miss Marshall's and the third room was the Headmaster's top class. Between these two rooms was a dividing screen, which pushed back and made one large room. I only remember it being one room for one occasion.

I had been asked to sing in front of the whole school. I chose to sing, 'Oh Land of my Father's', 'Wales'. It had a chorus and was quite long and the teacher suggested some other song, but I liked 'Wales' so she said she would get a boy and a girl to each sing a verse, which was much better. I was about six years old and I think two big boys pushed the screen back, so that they could all see us.

The whole school assembled in the large room and John Appleyard, Connie Bates and I sang 'Wales'. Nothing else, no one said anything, we all just filed back into our classrooms and the screen was pushed back. Connie Bates never forgot the experience. I was used to singing every week at Sunday school where the superintendent gave me a sweetie. It was no big event for me as I was used to singing.

In the baby class I don't remember writing on paper. I think we wrote on the walls on special places that had blackboards. I can remember slates and slate pencils, and chalk and shells for counters. The shells were small and cream coloured and my cousin Vera pushed one up her nose. She suggested I should push one up my nose and we'd see who could push it the furthest. I didn't fancy doing it as I thought it would hurt my nose. Vera got hers stuck and it wouldn't come down. The teacher sent for the Headmaster. He gave Vera his big handkerchief and told her to blow her nose, but it didn't budge. They were deciding to send her to hospital in an ambulance, but I think the teacher got it out with a buttonhook. It was very upsetting and Vera was crying. My cousin was just a little older than I.

I remember another incident when I was in the baby class at Clifton School. I had a drummer boy brooch. It was a free gift when you sent a coupon from Drummer Dyes back to them. I loved this brooch and one day in the porch cloakroom on the coat next to mine was my brooch. I unpinned it and put it on my coat. The little girl, of course, said it was hers and I insisted it was mine. She ran home and brought her mother to our house. I arrived home just before them and was absolutely amazed to see my brooch on the pincushion which hung in the corner by the fireplace. I thought there was only one drummer boy brooch. Mom calmed the other mother down and explained. She then gave me a long lecture on never taking so much as a pin from anybody.

In the baby class we had small chairs and some seats that were fastened to a desk to hold a few children. The seats tipped up, folded up, when not in use. The teacher's chair was plain wood, seat and back, with a fancy shape cut out on the back. I remember running my finger round it once when being nursed by Miss Pratt.

The room had a big coal fire to keep us warm. There was a high mantle shelf and a big fireguard. Everything seemed very big and maybe it was just that I was small at the time. Any lunch break apples or other fruit had to be put up on the mantle shelf. People didn't have sweets very often. We only had sweets at weekends.

I was very small for my age. My sister Kath was two years younger than I and very unhappy when I started school, as we had always played together. As Mom was expecting another baby arrangements were made for

Kath to come with me to school although she was only three years old. Because Kath was only three the teacher said she could come just when she wanted. Kath always loved school.

One day we were late, and upset, crying as we ran. The school door had a large iron ring, which was too heavy for us to turn – we knew we'd be locked out. As we ran along the road an elderly man pushing a wheelbarrow asked why Kath was crying. I tried to explain we thought we'd be late for school. He said, "I'll give her a ride in my wheelbarrow, that will cheer her up". He walked very slowly and made us much, much later. He was a lovely kind man, very plump and small. I think he collected manure in that wheelbarrow, but Kath was no worse for her ride. A big boy heard our frantic knocking on the school door and let us in. It all ended happily.

When I was about eight or nine years old the R101 airship flew over our school. We all heard this big noise and the headmaster came into my class and told Harry Quarmby to ring the fire bell. I didn't wait to do the drill. I just ran to Kath's classroom, flung open the door – the teacher's mouth fell open – and grabbed Kath who was sitting quite near. I said, "Come on Kath" and we dashed out, through the cloakroom and out into the yard in time to see the R101. We were the only two who did see it as it went behind a cloud. The boy rang the fire bell and everyone marched in file out of the school to the other door, and never saw the R101. We didn't know what it was; it looked like a huge oval balloon.

When you got into Mrs Squires' class at Clifton school the girls knitted pink vests. A cord went round the neck with two pompoms to draw it up high. I knitted one but I didn't want to wear it. Fortunately a girl who couldn't knit very well asked to buy it. In the next class we did sewing. Miss Marshall was not very good at cutting out. Nothing ever fitted. I learnt to knit before I went to school.

I always looked after Kath, and one day she had done some poor sewing and had had the cane. Kath showed me her hand at playtime. There was a red weal across it and I just felt so cross and took her in to school to the teacher who had punished her. Miss Marshall was a very nice teacher I thought and I was quite horrified that she had hurt my sister. I said, "Look what you've done to my sister's hand". It must have really impressed Miss Marshall and she never ever caned Kath again. Kath thought I was wonderful. We didn't tell my Mom. In those days if you got caned and told your parents they gave you another telling off. They always stood up for the teachers, well except one mother who once came to school because her daughter, who had St Vitus' Dance, had been caned.

We were quite shocked when Mrs Payne said, "Fetch me that cane ..." and she broke it across her knee and handed it to the Headmaster. He had at least another dozen canes in a cupboard, but she had made her point. Mom used to say, "Well you must have deserved it" if we said we'd been caned. Both Kath and I got caned most paint days. We did pictures and painted them Tuesdays and Thursdays if I remember right. Once I painted an ivy leaf and she said, "Two small, draw another round it". I did and then got the cane because the veins on the leaf weren't right, because of the alteration.

One girl called Mabel Hemsworth had trouble with her bladder and needed to go to the toilet quite often. Mrs Squire told her she must wait, but Mabel's mother had told her what she must do if this happened again. Mabel left her seat and went out to the front by the teacher's desk, pulled down her knickers, cronked on the floor and weed a large puddle round Mrs Squire's feet. It was very traumatic. Mrs Squire didn't cane her or anything.

When we went to the baths it was about a mile and a half at least from school. We walked; no one came with us. Sometimes we went from home after lunch depending on the time of the lesson. Mrs Cockroft taught us to swim. I thought she lived at the baths, but of course she didn't, she worked there! She rarely spoke and looked very stern, but she certainly knew how to teach us to swim and got everybody off swimming in a very short time.

The last person back from swimming got the cane. Mom baked beautiful currant teacakes on swimming days; the whole tabletop was covered with bread, rolls, twists, loaves, cobs and teacakes. The whole lot had to last a week. Cousin Hilda called every week after swimming and risked the cane; so did my sister Kath!

My cousin Nellie didn't wait to learn to swim, but went to the baths during the summer holidays. She jumped in from the top diving board into the deep, 6 ft end of water, and then did a dog paddle movement until she got to the side steps and climbed out. She went straight up again to the top board and jumped again. That's all she did all the time. She had no fear at all. Later she learned to swim of course and became a good swimmer.

Mary, centre, with Auntie Lucy, Uncle Frank, Nellie and Douglas Robinson

The desks in Mrs Squire's class, Miss Marshall's and Mr Firth's all had inkwells. A boy came round as monitor to fill each inkwell. The pens were plain wood and the nibs pushed in at the top. Paper was very precious and each page in an exercise book was folded into four sections. Sums were written in these columns. At Grammar School we had to set the sums out in the middle of the page, which seemed very, very wasteful. Eventually pens became more colourful, made of plastic, I suppose, with a flattened end to be used as a letter opener.

When we were at Clifton school a rag and bone man came to the school gates before dinner and waited until 1.30 for us to bring him rags, old clothes. He promised to give us a goldfish and he never did. We never brought him enough for a fish. I think I got a balloon once.

Occasionally a man came to school with a dummy. He wasn't very good. His mouth was moving all the time the dummy was talking. He had an artificial leg, a peg leg, which was very fascinating. He once sent word he would come, and then he didn't. I remember feeling so disappointed; I'd really built up on seeing him. He could walk so well with this wooden stump, it was more interesting than watching his mouth saying 'a gottle o' geer.'

In summer evenings we were taught country dancing on a lovely flat lawn behind the Armytage Arms, a public house across from our house and near the large gas lamp where we congregated. A lady who lived in part of the Armytage Arms trained us, and had an old gramophone and all the proper records for country dancing. She even managed to get young boys to dance. She trained us to do the maypole also. This place where we danced was right next to the part with the pond where Isobel once fell in.

The local blacksmith was in this part also. We used to go and watch him shoe horses. He must have been a farrier. He had two daughters and a son and they all lived along a country track. They had to get water from a well. Their house was very cosy, and very isolated and there was a duck pond quite near. We had all learnt to swim at an early age because Clifton had lots of streams and ponds, and Mom thought if we fell in we'd be better if we could swim. Isobel was the only one to fall in as I remember.

I loved fishing and used to go off every day, but I didn't fish in there, as there was nothing to catch; only sticklebacks and they didn't survive long. I never caught even them. The best place for fishing was another quarter of a mile further up the wagon lines where there was a really wonderful colony of newts. Great crested newts, some with gorgeous orange spots on their underbellies, lovely large newts with wonderful crests. I exercised them every day on my hands.

CHAPTER 4

Food and Fear and Folk

Dot was my eldest sister. We looked up to Dot. She was so clever, and she could make lovely food. She made the recipes up herself. She knew what would be right, adding unusual things. We had nasturtium leaves in salad, and dandelion, and pineapple on ham, and sweet and sour things, and beautiful scotch pancakes, out of this world. We made ice cream when there was snow outside. It was never a big success though.

We always made poppilolly at Easter time I think, and kept it down the cellar to come darker coloured. We always had pancakes on pancake Tuesday. If we forgot at lunchtime we'd have them for tea. Mom had a huge frying pan. We needed equipment that covered for a large family. The meat and potato dish was very big as I remember, and what delicious food we had always. No added colouring, flavouring or anything other than the good wholesome food. We didn't grow big and tall or fat. Kath was plump, and the rest of us quite skinny for most of our lives, and none of us were tall, but neither were Dad or Mom. We had lots of dairy produce. All the things that now are said to be bad for us. Cream and eggs and butter. We never ate margarine on our bread.

When I was seven I got mumps and was away from school for two weeks. When I went back the teacher said I'd gone back too soon, and sent me home, along with another little girl called May. We played together and enjoyed the extra week holiday.

One afternoon we took my sister Nora out in her pram. We walked along Thornhills Lane and a young man walked behind us for a while, and then walked with us. He had his thumb wrapped up. He said someone had thrown a big doll over the wall, and did we want to go for it, he would show us where it was. Of course we said yes, and went with him across a field to the top of the railway side. We looked over the wall, but there was no dolly. He then said he wanted to wee, but he couldn't unfasten his trousers, as he had a bandage on, and asked May if she could help him. He said, "have you ever seen a boy?" and I said, "No" but May had a cousin, so he let May help with his buttons.

I realised it wasn't right, so picked up Nora and put her in the pram and said, "We have to go now, we are going to our Auntie Lottie's for tea", and I ran with the pram all the way home, pushing a heavy pram up the steep hill, and leaving May without a qualm. All I thought of was getting away, and the awful thought that I'd told a lie.

We weren't going to Auntie Lottie's. That really worried me. So I told Mom when I got home and she told the police. When the policeman came they spoke outside, not in front of me. They didn't want to upset me.

Many years later my sister Kath was abused walking home from visiting me at Hove Edge. This man followed her and eventually tried to grab her. She yelled so loud, she woke a man, in a house nearby, who pushed up his bedroom window and said, "I'm coming lass", and pulled on his trousers over his pyjamas and came and chased this awful man. Talking about this brought Mom to thinking of my earlier experience and I said, "Yes, Bobby Rutter came, and you talked on the step", and Mom was amazed. She thought I didn't know.

May by the way wasn't harmed. I looked back and saw him leave May and go back up the field, unwinding the bandage, which was his hankie. We knew where he lived, but no one asked us. He was never summoned. We never forgot though.

One well-known character in my youth was Violet. She was a lovely person. When she had a form to fill in she brought it always to the little sweet shop at the end of our terrace. The lady there, Mrs Tattersall, would help her. She would say, "Fill in the date there". Violet would say, "What is it?" Mrs Tattersall said "October". "How do I spell October?" said Violet. "O" said Mrs Tattersall.

"How do I spell O?" said Violet. Then Mrs Tattersall took over. Woolworth's came to Brighouse and wanted lots of people to serve on in the store. Violet and her little friend Emily both went to apply. They were unsuccessful. Violet was very put out, and said "What did they want, a beauty chorus?" Violet collected empty wooden boxes from stalls in the market, and from shops, and chopped and bundled them up and sold them for fire lighting. She had a fleet of prams.

Another character was Friend. He couldn't attend school, but went to a special school for quite a while. When he came back home he told my Grandma he was now a tailor. "Oh can you make a suit?" she said. "No Mrs Baldwin I can't make suits". "Oh do you make jackets?" "No Mrs Baldwin I don't make jackets". "Do you make trousers or waistcoats?" "No Mrs Baldwin I don't make trousers or waistcoats. But you know those two tapes at the back of the waistcoats, I can sew those on". Friend seemed able to find himself jobs, and the last one was at a bakery. One Friday afternoon he dropped a custard and the manager said he could take it home for his mother. He dropped one every Friday afternoon after that.

There was another gentleman, also called Friend, living in the village, who cleared all the grates. If we lost a penny down the grate and went to Friend's house, he would bring his scoop and walk to the grate however far away, and empty it and find the coin. When he met me he always said "Marjorie Parjory, teapot knob, goes to bed at seven o'clock". Then to my little sister Isobel he said "Is a bell necessary on a bicycle". Friend's mother spoke very Yorkshire and one day when the vicar was visiting her she said they should put the King and Kaiser in a field, give them both a blather, and let them fuffen it out, to settle the first war. Well, it would have saved a few million lives if they had.

Friend had a sister, Miss Brooke. Very stern and quite forbidding really, but I said I would knit her a jumper. I never did, but she always seemed more pleasant after that. I had just learned to cast on.

Another character was Miss Griggs. She sold eggs. When she came round in an evening Mom always invited her in, and when Mom paid her she always turned her back and bent right down, so I ran round once just in time to see her putting the money in a purse down the top of her stocking. Miss Griggs always wore a large straw hat. She had a lot of hair which she pushed up inside her hat. She lived at Ox Close, a smallholding where everything was very clean. Even the pig was clean.

The people who owned the Armytage Arms also had a row of pigsties, all with large pigs, some with a litter. We went to look at the pigs on a Sunday afternoon after Sunday school. I took my cousins too and put a leaf of

ivy down the neck of our dresses to find out whom we'd
marry:

> Ivy, ivy I love thee
> Down my bosom I put thee
> The first young man to speak to me
> Shall be my loving husband.

CHAPTER 5

Exams and Brighouse Girls Grammar School

I remember very well the day I sat for the county minor exam. In those days you had two chances. The first try was Junior, for people who were younger so that if they failed they still had time to take the exam again, and then that was the Senior County Minor.

A few months prior to this date I had been an attendant for the Rose Queen on Demonstration Day in Brighouse. It was a Trades procession, and brass band and landaus for the Queen and attendants. I would have been ten years old and the other girl, who was also ten, was taking the county minor at the same time as I was. Her aunt and my aunt were friends, and told us to look out for each other. This little girl called Mary had brought egg sandwiches to eat in the break time, and she shared them with me. I was never a good eater, and never thought about food, but those egg sandwiches tasted very good. We had done the maths paper, and after the break it was the English test.

Author as attendant to Rose Queen, standing next to Rose Queen on left.

A man sat in front at a desk, which was raised up a little and all the desks in the room were set out with a big space around each one. The man kept a keen eye on everyone and of course we hadn't to talk. I remember leaving the essay question until I'd finished everything else. I liked essays and must have begun with speed which he noticed. He walked up the aisle as far as my desk, stood behind me reading what I'd put, then walked solemnly back to his desk. In a while he came again. It made me think he was liking to read my essay. I wrote things to make him laugh – playing to an audience. Being one of five you don't get a lot of individual attention. I loved the thought that he was finding it interesting. We had to write about a house we would like to live in. I wrote pages, very quickly, even describing the kitchen curtains blowing out of the open window. I described the garden, with a part to keep hens and a cockerel to waken me up in a morning.

When I'd finished one girl was still writing. She came from Clifton and I walked home with her. She had only answered one question, and not finished that. The question said "Complete four of the following" and there were 100 different two lines of poems. She had tried to do them all!

I told my eldest sister and Mom about the maths test and they realised I had put the point wrong on one answer. Dot said I'd not pass. I thought I'd got another wrong answer, it was about wallpaper and how many rolls would I need to paper a room given the measurements. They felt to be quite hard questions, and I think I'd made careless mistakes. However I passed and a boy from Clifton had also passed for the Boys' Grammar School. I think my English got me through.

When the results came to Clifton School the headmaster said I could go home to tell my parents, and Ralph also came with me to give the good news to his Mom. We walked up the road, and past where they were building a wall and big gate for the new cemetery. A herd of cows was being brought to a farm to be milked and they were all across the road and also on the pavement.

I was always a little nervous of cows ever since a kind farmer lifted me up onto a cow's back for a ride when I was very small. I got right up to the cemetery gate and hoped the cows would pass. Ralph had gone through the herd then realised I wasn't with him, and he came back and grabbed my hand. He was fed up with me and wanted to get home quickly to tell his Mom he'd passed. I thought he was the bravest of the brave to take me through those cows.

So I was the second one to go to Grammar School. Dot should have left at the end of the summer term and I was to begin in September. There were no jobs at the time, so Dot went back to school for another year. She was very, very clever. I felt full of confidence going to a new school with my sister already there. No problem for me.

I had only been there three weeks when I got threatened with expulsion. I was walking home with about five big girls. I knew two of them only. They were discussing the raid we had just had on the cloakroom. Staff came unannounced and we had to stand by our lockers and bring everything out for inspection to check that they were named. Every single item had to be marked with our names. We bought nametapes, and had had to sew them on everything – shoes were marked with a pen. One of these five girls said Betty Tattersall had marked her scarf after the raid had started. She was a prefect and my sister's friend, and marking a scarf during a raid was considered very bad. She lived near us and I was in the bath that night and Betty came and sat talking to me. I said, "You shouldn't have marked your scarf". I think she was worried that I knew and must have decided to tell the Head. Maybe she didn't mark it I don't know, but the Head Mistress got me out of my class and walked me to different classrooms asking me to find the girl who had said Betty Tattersall marked her scarf.

Well I kept going up to a certain girl saying it was she, but it wasn't this Dorothy, although she was there as one of the five girls. The girl who had actually said it was too scared to own up. I didn't know what all the fuss was about. They put Dorothy in different rooms and I always went to her each time. Miss Scott was a huge lady and very stern, but I held her hand when we went round the school. Eventually she brought all the sixth form and prefects into her study and sent for me. They were all standing in two rows. I walked down the middle of them. My sister Dot was one of them and felt very ashamed of me I suppose even though I wasn't really understanding what it was all about. Miss Scott kept saying if I didn't find the right girl she would expel me and the girl I kept accusing promised on Guides' honour, she had not said Betty Tattersall had marked her scarf.

I walked home with Dot and she said, "Next time you are sent for to go to Miss Scott's study, don't walk in as though you own the place". I was just puzzled with it all. I was 52.5 lbs in weight and 52.5 inches tall. They said a pound for every inch. Eleven years old and under four stones in weight. I don't see how a girl so small could walk in looking as though she owned the head mistress's study. Fortunately the real culprit summoned up her courage and admitted she had been the one. The whole matter just fizzled out. Miss Scott frightened most people, but fortunately I was never nervous of people, just cows.

Miss Scott, four years later, walked up the hockey field looking at every one as she passed by. We were supposed to be reading poetry, sitting under shady trees. I had been talking to my friend Vera. Miss Scott stopped in front of me. I thought, "How could she possibly know I'd been talking instead of reading?" We were at the far end of the hockey field. She beckoned me to go with her. She wanted me to go to Brighouse Station to meet a lady guest who was coming to stay with her. She said "Oh and offer to carry her case of course". I said "Yes Miss Scott" and off I went.

I wondered how I'd know which lady was the visitor, then thought she might be the only one with a case. I had my school cap and uniform on of course, and this very nice motherly lady came up to me, so no problem. Her case was very big and she wouldn't hear of me carrying it. I doubt if I could have lifted it. I talked to her all the way back to school. Miss Scott lived almost next door, within a hundred yards of the school. We had Vespers on Fridays and the guest was on the platform with Miss Scott. She was looking at everyone, until she spotted me and we had a little wave. I think I'd told her all my family history. I think she had come from Germany and I wondered afterwards if she was a Jewess escaping before the war. It would be 1935, so maybe not.

Although we did have German girls coming over that were pen pals. I had written to Etheltraud Lauter for two years, and then we'd given up writing. After two more years this group came to school so I asked one of them if they knew Etheltraud Lauter, and I pronounced it all wrongly, and after looking puzzled this girl said "Ah you mean Trowdel Lowter. She is here." She had come as the guest of another girl, who was in our sixth form. Etheltravd looked a very mature woman about 5 ft 5 inches and maybe nine stones in weight, maybe more. I had been thinking of her as my size because she was my age. I felt I'd written ridiculous letters, childish, of course they wanted to learn to write and speak English, and that was why they had asked for pen friends.

Friedeline Wagner also paid us a long visit in 1931. She was the granddaughter of the famous Wagner. She had her hair in plaits, and she pulled her left hand plait and her tongue popped out to the left of her mouth, and then pulled her other plait and her tongue shot over to the right. She pulled her nose and her tongue shot back inside her mouth. She did all this while the teacher was writing on the board. She was a little buckstick really.

When we were first year students we did cookery and also learned how to serve lunch. Quite a number of girls stayed every day as they lived quite a distance from school. One table was for the staff and two of the teachers helped to serve. There was a hatch through to the kitchen and two ladies always cooked a lovely dinner. I have mentioned about my height etc before, well I stood at the open hatch and Mrs Sparkes handed me a large size turkey dish, piled high with fishcakes. I was supposed to carry this across and put it on a large sideboard made of drawers, but it just dropped straight down and crashed onto the floor!

Poor Mrs Sparkes. She picked the fishcakes off the floor, and rescued as many as she could, the ones that weren't too broken and which were on top of others. She then went across to the staff room and told them that one of the servers had dropped the dinner. I was serving the staff table and Miss Ashby was helping. She said to me, "I wonder which one of the servers it was who dropped the dinner". I said it was me, and she said, "I thought so". I cheered up though when all the servers got lashings of fishcakes, squashed and broken, but they tasted just as good, and usually there wasn't much left for servers. It didn't worry me at all anyway because I ate like a sparrow. The day I dropped them one of the teachers took the water jug from me saying she didn't trust me with that round her back, and she filled up all the glasses on the table. She smiled when she said it. They really took it all in good part. No one drops all the dinner on purpose do they?

When I went to the Grammar School the art teacher was very good. She asked us questions about creation. I knew all the answers, coming from St John's Clifton, with having had scriptures every day. Miss Ashby said I mustn't answer any more questions. We had to paint the creation. I did creatures like newts coming out of the sea onto the land. The sky came out a bit blotchy. Rather than add blue I decided to draw God looking down on His creation. Miss Ashby gave me 49/50 for my effort. When I thought of all the times I had had the cane for art, it was a very nice feeling. I was the monitor and the next test was about points of vision, perspective etc. I was busy giving out the paper and pencils etc and didn't hear any of the lesson. We had the test; everyone was given two pieces of paper. We had to draw a box. I was hopeless, and she said, "You only did one Marjorie". "Oh no", I said, "I did two". I had done the other on the back to save paper. At Clifton we had to be very careful always and save paper. Miss Ashby looked at my second attempt, which was no better than my 1st, so she gave me 10/50. I never did learn about perspective. I wish now I had. Anything with imagination and I could do alright, but I was never any good at copying. Ah well, we can't have it all ways.

One of Marjorie's own paintings. She has painted her own cards for many years now, painting landscapes, often with snow and always with two birds flying past.

For gym lessons we wore pale blue, poplin dresses, very short, with knickers to match. These gym lessons were a Government sponsored initiative to get the nation fit during the period before the Second World War. During my first gym lesson, the teacher, Miss Maclaughlin, said, "Has anyone climbed a rope?" I said, "I have climbed a gas lamp". So I had first try and got right up to the ceiling. I loved gym, if it wasn't jumping over the buck, or the box. Being small I couldn't do those high things. I was always a team leader in gym and after I left Grammar School and joined an evening keep fit class run by the same mistress, I was team leader there too!

I wasn't very good at sports. In hockey I could dribble the ball up the wing quite quickly, but wasn't good at centring it. I did get as far as a trial for the school team, however. I remember during the game a flock of wild geese flew over in a V shape and I stopped to watch them and held up the game. They decided I was no good! Even so, the whole five years I was elected form leader every time. The form mistress chose me the first time, as she knew Dot. After that the form voted.

The second year I fell off my bicycle, at least, Bessie, my friend, came too close and got her pedal in my front wheel. We were at the bottom of John King in Brighouse. A lorry was following slowly and managed to stop and a big girl called Boocock picked me up. I could not get up myself. I could see the lorry's wheels. They carried me into the chemist's and gave me sal volatile. Miss Young, our science and maths teacher and my very favourite, got a taxi and brought me home. I can see our Nora's face now. She opened the front door, then folded her arms and said, "What have you come to this door for?" quite ignoring Miss Young. Mum had given us a lecture only that lunchtime about not coming to the front door and bringing dirt through, we'd to use the back. Poor Nora was only seven years old and that was why she gave the unwelcome greeting to Miss young. Luckily Mom came and got me inside, but I couldn't walk again for three weeks. My knee got cured with Ellerman's Horse liniment. An old man at Church told Dad it would get rid of the fluid. It did, but how painful. It blistered my skin and I had to have it on twice a day. I missed an important few weeks at school. Because I'd passed the Junior County Minor exam I was younger than most in the class. They were going to keep me down to do the work again, including what I'd missed, but then decided to put me up halfway into Lower IVB. I would do the work I'd missed which was what mattered.

So I was put in the B stream and I loved it. From then on I was always top or second. There was a girl exactly as clever as me. Our final grade would be within 1%. If she was top, I was second, if I was top she was second. When I took my report home my parents always said, "Well Marj, you are the best of a bad lot". Well that was because I liked being top and must have been showing off. Dot and Kath were always near the top too, but one girl always beat Kath. They didn't want me to get thinking I was more clever than Dot or Kath. That's why they said, "Best of a bad lot", because it was B stream.

Dot took two Civil Service exams and came fourth and seventh position in all England, top in Geography. The Geography teacher at school was so excited. She always gave me good marks thinking I'd be like Dot. I became a perfectionist. Always feeling I should try harder, and never feeling satisfied. I left school in 1935. Dot had been with me until 1931. She stayed on an extra year, as there was a shortage of jobs. Dot began in 1925. Isobel left in 1947 and there was one of us there continuously for 22 years, usually two together. They had never had 5 sisters before or since so put a special item in the school magazine when Isobel left to say "the last of the Sutcliffes."

We had a Scientific and Geographic Society and a Literary Society. I joined all there was. A professor came from Leeds once to give a talk about birds. He was very interesting. I was form leader, and had to always help anyone coming to school giving talks. This man had a lot of things to bring in from his vehicle, stuffed birds mostly; and he had bird warblers, he gave me one, which was supposed to be a robin. It was a simple thing to make. I think wood, a washer of leather and a nail. He knew all about birdcalls.

I gave two talks, one by myself about Robin Hood and Hartshead. My Uncle Albert provided a lot of information. He was a wood carver, and worked always from home. I loved to go watch, and see all the mess he made with the floor covered with wood shavings. Auntie Gertie, his wife, was very kind and patient. Uncle Albert always argued and loved to talk about Russia. He became disillusioned though, when he got very old.

Uncle Albert Baldwin with the long case clock he carved and donated to Brighouse Library.

Well, Uncle Albert lent me lots of picture slides of the Saxon and Norman parts of Hartshead Church and pictures of Robin Hood's grave in Kirklees Park. The room where I had to give the talk had seats rising from the front, so the back row was near the ceiling. We had this Magic Lantern, and all the windows had black curtains. I hadn't brought a torch. I couldn't remember whether it was a rounded window for the Saxon part or a pointed. I just guessed and hoped no one would know. When the lights went on I checked and my luck was in, I'd got it right, just by chance. I don't know why I got asked to do those lectures.

The one for the Scientific Society was the best enjoyed by the audience. I did it with a girl called Molly. She lived at Lightcliffe and knew a gentleman who did magic tricks. He spent an evening with us and we called our talk Black Magic. Molly's tricks all turned out right. I wasn't just as good. The first one was with a hard-boiled egg. My Mom gave me one for the lecture, but couldn't spare one for a practice at home, so I had never tried it. You took the shell off then plunged a lighted paper into an empty salad cream jar, plonked the egg on top while the paper was burning, and it was supposed to have made a vacuum and would suck the egg into the jar. Fortunately it was my first trick. I just had to leave it sitting on top of the salad cream bottle and it looked as though nothing had happened. We had a very nice science mistress and every time I looked at her for approval, after finishing my talks.

Because I had always loved fishing I used to go off every day to catch frogs, newts, crayfish, beetles, dragon fly larvae, pond skaters, water boatmen, cadis worms etc. I was asked to organise the aquarium at Grammar School. The hobby lasted me right until I left at 16. I had a most wonderful aquarium in the lab, and cleared it and kept it stocked the whole five years. I went two or three times a week through all the holidays to feed the stock and clean out the tank which we placed outside in the shade, where we had a tap for watering the gardens. I had a piece of fine mesh to cover the tank top and put a pebble on to weight it down. Once I forgot the pebble and two newts got out. They even got out of the Lab and went walking down the corridor. Two lady cleaners thought they were baby crocodiles and one lady became hysterical and said that she'd never clean the top corridor again, but she did!

CHAPTER 6

Playing Out; Friends, Enemies and Bicycles!

No one had a car in Clifton except Sir George Armytage, Mr Balmforth and later Mr Lister. Children played in the road. Hopscotch, skipping, cricket etc, kick can and hook it and tennis, with a chalk line for the net and a ribbon round our foreheads, pretending to be Susan Longlan and Betty Nuttall.

After school we used to play round a large gas lamp in the middle of the road. One night in Winter a big group had gathered and one boy was playing a harmonica, he was a real expert. A young boy my age said, "Tell him to shut up!"

I called out, "A penny for you to play in the next street!" He was wearing clogs and when he chased me sparks came out of his clogs. I ran for my life and in the wrong direction, away from home. Fear put wings to my feet. He didn't catch me. I waited a while and then came back and he didn't say anything.

I remember going chumping for bonfire night with big boys and girls. They got a big tree which had fallen. They fastened a rope round it and dragged it back on the road. They gave me a ride and I sat on it. When we were almost back home the village policeman came on his bicycle. All the boys dropped the rope and ran off leaving me sitting on the tree. The nice policeman just laughed and put his book and pen in his pocket and rode off.

We had wonderful bonfires although I never liked banging fireworks. One of Dad's violin pupils was a joiner in his father's business and bought all his nails etc at a shop in Brighouse, who also sold fireworks in October and November. When the shop was ready to close on bonfire night this pupil always went in and the shop keeper gave him a large box of fireworks which he always brought to our house, and we had a lovely display in our back garden.

We played marbles at a certain time of year. I don't know what decided it, but everyone played; suddenly it was marble time. We bought them from the little shop. Lucy Bottomley won them from us. She had stone jars on her mother's cellar shelf full of marbles. She really was an expert. Everyone was marble mad for a time then it moved onto something else, maybe cricket, or skipping. I could never do Diablo. My Mom knew how, and she also showed us how to play jacks. These were small squares of porcelain and were picked up after bouncing a little ball, first one then two then three.

Marjorie, second from right on the front row, with her friends.

When we were young, boys had metal bully bowls with a metal hooked rod to make it run along the ground. Blacksmiths would make them. To start it off they hung the hoop with the hooked rod at the bottom, and then let it drop to the ground and give it a push keeping the hooked rod on the metal ring. Girls had wooden bully bowls, and hit them with a rod of wood. They were larger in circumference than the boys' metal bully bowls. It was always nice if a boy let you have a turn on his metal hoop. Not often that happened. We also got long bamboo rods, which had been used for curtain hanging maybe. We pretended to be Girl Guides, and wore our school caps sideways, with the points at front and back instead of the points to right and left. We marched about with these poles then ran and jumped with them. I remember winding myself once on one. We didn't play at it again after that, although still had the Girl Guide Patrol for quite a long time. It was a secret society, and we had secret signs to do before we could enter the cycle shed, which was our headquarters.

I loved flying a kite when I was small. I had a yellow one, and it kept diving down to earth. A friend of Dad's tied a sod to the tail, and it then flew quite safely. When I went to Cromer at 14 years, I bought a box kite. We flew it on the beach. Nothing nicer than lying in the sun, just gently pulling the string of a kite letting it go higher and higher on a lovely sunny day. Cromer had six weeks of glorious weather; it only rained once, during Sunday dinner. The season was only six weeks, and the whole town had to make enough money to keep them the rest of the year. Prices were much higher than at Blackpool. Cromer was posh. When I was there a little man, who had a bad limp, came with a zither and played on the cliff top. I followed him to the next village. He wore a brown suit and brown boots. He was very small in stature, maybe with being lame. He could certainly play the zither. He struck the strings with canes bent round at the end. He placed his cap on the ground for people to put coins in. I don't think he got a lot, but it was lovely weather and he was very suntanned. Lots of musicians had to go busking in those days. Talkies had come and orchestras in cinemas were all disbanded. Our Dad always kept his day job, so we didn't suffer like some of the families of musicians.

Skipping was always a good exercise. We'd get a long rope if a clothesline had broken, or a plaited straw rope from the greengrocer's cart, and skip in the road for hours. No traffic of course, only the occasional horse and cart.

Once a cruel man was beating his horse, to make it pull its heavy load, and Mrs Greenwood was so incensed she went out to him and took his whip off him and hit him with it. She was a very genteel lady, and spoke with a southern accent. She was very brave to tackle this uncouth man. We often told of this incident to Isobel, my youngest sister, who was only a little child at the time. As she grew up Isobel thought she herself had been the heroine, and her three daughters were told this story.

We had a cycle shed in our back garden, which also held the peggy tubs for washday. It became our Girl Guide Secret Society. I had a metal box with a key to lock it, and scratched the word PRIVET, never being good at spelling. The shame of that box! Everyone was always remarking about it when I got older! That it should have been 'PRIVATE'. We kept a list of the rules in the box. One girl who lived in the back of Kiln Fold was not allowed to be a member. I don't think she'd ever have wanted to be anyway. We used to run away if we saw her coming. She was as strong as a boy. Her Mom was a Cockney. They were comers-in.

About this time a little girl called Alice died of pneumonia. Mom said she'd played in the wet grass and not changed her clothes and it made her poorly. My cousin took me to look at Alice laid in her cot. Her face so clean, and her hair with blue ribbons. She looked so peaceful and her Dad was sitting by her side with his head in his hands. He said, "She's asleep". I said, "No, she's dead". My cousin kept taking different children to see her. She looked so beautiful. She'd be five, maybe, no maybe three. She was in a cot, so couldn't have been older than three. She was my age.

Mom had help in the house. A lady to help with the washing Mondays and another came Friday to clean. Mrs Wood the cleaner also worked for the vicar who had a daughter. I was once invited to the vicarage to play with "Baby" Sherlock and have tea. When I went back home I had to choose a toy – anything I wanted. There was a train that ran on a round track, and wonderful dolls etc. I thought I'd better choose the least expensive thing and it was a wooden man hanging from a bar. You turned a handle and he acrobated over the bar. Mrs Wood was very pleased with me and took me back home. We'd had tea in the nursery, just Baby and me, not with her Mum and Dad. I felt sorry for her, no sisters and by herself in such a big house. She was called Baby as long as she lived in Clifton, and she was a very big girl. Many years later we tried to buy the vicarage, but didn't get it fortunately. The work would have been too much. It was when we retired and wished to live in Clifton again. It was big enough for Kath and her husband Ray, and me and Eric and our eldest sister Dot. We thought it would be like our own nursing home, but it wasn't to be.

I remember just once Dad taking Kath and me to Clifton school, when the weather was very windy. We had a war memorial on the village green and I had misheard that a boy had been lifted right over the top of the war memorial so that was why Dad was walking with us. Actually it was the boy's cap that had gone over the war memorial only. I imagined him up in the air flying.

Another frightening instance stays in my mind. Friday afternoon the headmaster read a story to us, very dramatically. It was Treasure Island, and I was listening very intently, and he said about this pressgang coming and tap, tap, tap. At this identical Moment I heard tap, tap, tap out in the playground and I was petrified. I hardly dared go home, but found workmen were mending the school gate fixing a catch on a block of stone to hold the gate open.

When we were very young and wanted a friend to stay overnight, we used to make the bed up the other way, so that we all slept across the bed and there was plenty of room then for the extra person. We always slept two to a double bed anyway. I curled up so I was never popular except as a teller of stories, and for making midnight feasts. We read tales of boarding schoolgirls having midnight feasts, so I suppose that gave us the idea. We liked to have a torch under the bedclothes and make a tent. We were usually all asleep before nine o'clock.

The time when Isobel fell in the pond was very upsetting. We had only one fishing net and at that time our friend Bessie Gill was using it. I was next to her, and then Kath, then Nora and Isobel at the end. She had to lean right out over this pond to see what we were doing, and she fell in of course. When she surfaced we pulled her out, all covered in a horrible smelling black mud. We went straight home, but made Isobel walk on the other side of the road because of the smell. We were soon back home. It was a very warm summer's day. Mom undressed Isobel out on the back flags, and put her in a bath of water, and put all her clothes in the dustbin. A friend of Mom's was paying us a visit at the time; we were very relieved, and didn't get into trouble for letting Isobel fall in.

When I was three or four I often visited the lady who lived in the top house of our terrace. She was beautiful, with white curly hair. Her legs and body were very small, like a child's. Tiny feet. She always sat on the floor, and when she went out, very occasionally, she went in a bath chair. She taught me to knit, and I spent many happy hours with her. When she'd had me long enough she slapped her hands on the floor as though chasing me off, and I knew to run home. She showed me how to sew and thread a needle and kept saying if at first you don't succeed, try, try, try again. I was trying, and I nearly used to cry sometimes.

Once I was there and the vicar was paying a visit. I ran under the table which had a chenille cover down to the carpet. I was just in time. Mrs Nicholson and her daughter Jennie knew I was there, and they never told the vicar thinking he would only stay ten minutes which was the usual time for his visit, and he stayed half an hour. I never made a sound, and came out when he'd gone. They were so terrified I might sneeze or move the cover, and shock the vicar, but all was well.

I did have to go to bed once as a punishment. It was when I was 15. I was at Grammar School and we were to have a holiday the following day, for Princess Marina's wedding day. We were told to listen on the wireless to the ceremony, and then we would then have to write an essay about it when we returned to school. At teatime our Nora had been teasing me, on and on, and I lost my patience and said in front of my Mum and Dad, "You are a devil". They looked at me askance, and I said, "She is". Dad said "Up those stairs, and you stay there, and all day tomorrow". That's the last time I swore. Writing essays was quite nice I thought, usually, but that one I had to write was the very poorest essay I ever did. I got 6/10. I hadn't heard any of it, and just asked questions about it going to school from three other girls.

I used to help the neighbour at the bottom house who had a baby boy. She thought babies' bottles were unhygienic and he was fed with a spoon, from a cup. It was thin gruel, and he was laid on a pillow on the floor. It took ages to feed him, and it was almost time for the next feed.

He was a lovely little boy and later when I was 14 years old I went to Cromer by myself for six weeks to care for Tommy – he suffered from hay fever and the idea was to play with him on the beach where there was no pollen. I went again the following year for the whole of the summer holiday, six weeks. Those journeys on the train, alone, and changing five times, sometimes just changing platforms but once changing stations, and once going over a bridge, were very hazardous, but I had it all written down, and Mom came to Brighouse station to see me off. Her final words were "find a carriage with a lady in it and a child if possible". I nearly missed getting on the train once as I could only see elderly men. However,

I got safely to Cromer after a whole day's travelling, and it was a big adventure for me in those days.

Dot, who was five years older than me, worked as a dispenser and receptionist for a doctor at Mirfield for her first job. Mirfield is a few miles from Clifton so Dot had a bicycle. I remember the day Dot was brought home in a lorry with her broken cycle on the back. She was sometimes a bit of a dreamer, and she must have stopped concentrating on her bicycle and ridden into a herd of cows and ended up with her front wheel up a cow's back. Fortunately her bike wasn't very badly damaged and Dot was more shocked than anything. She was on her way to work but the kind lorry driver thought she should come back home, and brought her to the front door.

I often had Dot's old bikes, as she needed a reliable one to go to Mirfield twice a day for her job and had to keep getting newer ones. She did the doctor's income tax and looked after everything, made up medicines, and ran things when the doctor was out. Once she ordered an ambulance and sent a sick man to hospital. He said she saved his life. He had a burst ulcer. Dot knew how to look after us when we ailed things; in fact, I trusted her as though she was a qualified doctor. She was very clever.

Once when Dr Smith needed a six weeks break he got a locum in who was very new to general practice and he left a lot of it to Dot. He had to visit some of the patients so he took her with him. If there was any bandaging to be done he often said, 'I think you can do this better than I'. On one occasion she had to bandage a man's head. When the doctor was very busy she tried not to disturb him and saw to the regular patients herself.

The YHA was a new organisation at this time and I bought a bike from my friend so that Dot and I could go on a cycling holiday through the YHA. I wore bright red on my bicycle and I painted my bike red too. I called it the "Red Peril". Later it became "The Blue Peril". Our first trip was to Asenby near Topcliffe at Easter. Later we toured from Filey up to Saltburn and also the Lake District.

I had started my first job, a book keeper/cashier for a silk mill in Brighouse. I left school on the Friday and started work on the Monday. My 16th birthday was on the day before, so I didn't have a holiday. After three weeks the managing director said I could have a week off. The girl whose job I was learning was there, she taught me for six weeks. I hadn't saved for a holiday so set off with very little money. Mom paid for my bed, breakfast and evening meal at each hostel before we set off. The money I had was for lunch and tea each day. If I spent 1/- on lunch I had nine pence for tea. It worked out just right. I had nothing left when we got home. Dot and I saw the lovely countryside. Cycling was just right for seeing it all.

Walking felt we were looking too long at everything and car riding you went too fast and missed things.

Because I loved cycling I started a cycling club at the Tech, all the members except me were boys. One Whitsuntide holiday the weather was cold and there was a very strong wind, but it was not nice weather for cycling. We had gone to Malham Cove and climbed up Goredale Scar. The wind made it very hard to peddle back home. Even the boys were tired. I felt exhausted. My sister Kath came looking for me as we were late getting back home because of the wind. Kath pushed my bike up the hill home and half carried me too. Dot and Max had ridden from York and Dot had damaged her foot and couldn't press the pedal down, so came all the way having only one strong foot and lifting the other pedal up with her toe. It took many hours to get home. It was a Whitsuntide we always remembered.

Another of the Tech Cycling Club trips was to Boston Spa. When we got there we saw they had rowing boats on the river, and I went along with a boy for a row. There wasn't enough water in the river and the oars touched the bed of the river. We asked for our money back but we didn't get it. Often we cycled 100 miles in a day.

I went four times only as no more girls joined us. Once I really felt exhausted and a man who always accompanied us, and then put a report in the Brighouse

Echo, gave me a banana and saved my life I thought. I did have something wrong with my heart but didn't know I had, so I was lucky to survive the four trips with the Tech Cycling Club, as boys were able to cycle much faster than girls. They never left me, but I always tried to ride my fastest, and they were cruising along taking it easy.

During one trip we were having a rest and they started playing football. One boy grabbed the back of another boy's shorts and a piece of the material tore right out. They went to a house and asked the lady to repair the damage. Fortunately she managed to do a good job and he was able to cycle home looking decent.

CHAPTER 7

Music

Music was always part of our lives from an early age. Kath and I started when we were probably nine and seven years old, maybe even younger. Kath sang alto and it was that which caused people to be amazed. She stuck to the alto part so cleverly. We sang in most of the local churches and got invited to chapel events, pie suppers etc. We always wore white dresses. We once went to sing at our own church on the wrong Friday – we went a week early to this Friday meeting. We were very bashful sitting there in our white frocks, a week too soon.

Once I had tonsillitis and could not possibly sing. Kath kept coming upstairs to see if I was better. She said, "It's pork and apple sauce and seasoning, Marj, can't you get better?" Poor Kath couldn't go without me, with just singing alto. I could have gone and just sang a few solos but it wouldn't have been as good.

Marjorie, right with Kath.

For our Christmas present at this time Dot bought us a copy of Songs from Shakespeare's Plays, duets. We had to learn them all, and we had to do a dance in between the verses of "Gather Ye Rosebuds". Dot was a hard taskmaster sometimes. When she retired she taught children to play the piano. The parent of a mentally handicapped child said to me Dot was a saint. She had such a lot of patience. One of Dad's pupils was also backward, and Dad managed to teach him to play the violin. It's strange, but they felt it more rewarding, it must have been a real challenge.

We always sang in bed at night even after I'd left Clifton school. Kath taught me songs that she was learning at school so that we could still sing together. She always sang alto and I sang soprano. We always started with "Say from". That was a two-part song "Say from what golden quivers of the sky, do all thy winged arrows fly. Swiftness and power, by truth are thine, from thy great sire they came thy SIRE the word divine". At the time we didn't know what it meant. We liked the tune and the harmony, so sang it almost every night. We practised the two part songs Dot bought us too and always enjoyed just singing for ourselves.

Mom and Dad's friends were mostly musicians and came to our house for musical evenings. We were all put to bed early and this hoard of people came, all bringing their instruments. Dot was allowed to stay up to accompany on the piano. The man with the double bass had to come in last. He stood behind the door. We slept through it. We were brought up with it and it didn't disturb our sleep. How they all fitted in our lounge I'll never know. We didn't call it the lounge, it was the front room.

Our room fireplace originally had tiles in the hearth and round the fire too. Pictures, blue and white and some of the tiles had words saying, "The mill will never grind with the water that is past". I liked the pictures, but also remember the excitement of having a new fireplace. It had a high wood surround in polished oak, very grand. We had bookshelves under the window, and a big bookcase on one wall and a gramophone on top of a cabinet full of L.P. records.

We were the last family in Clifton to get a wireless. They were run from batteries of course, as electricity didn't arrive until 1949. Why we couldn't have a wireless was because the music wasn't suitable for us. Dad and Mom wanted us to appreciate good music first. When we knew and loved good music we could then listen to "rubbish" without it harming us. If we didn't know good music and only listened to the inferior sort, we would grow up thinking that was good. This was the explanation given to us when everyone else had a wireless except us. I went next door, and to the top house in the terrace, to listen to children's hour. The top house said it was a cat's whisker that made it play and I believed them. It all felt like magic.

Our music teacher at Grammar School was a lovely man. He had us singing different notes that he popped down on the piano to see if we could sing to pitch correctly. Well no problem for one who had done that from pram days. He then formed a choir. I loved that. One day he looked at my hand and said he would like to teach me the piano. I had small but long fingers. I told my Dad what he'd said. He charged quite a lot for lessons, so Dad said tell him if he likes to send Sylvia his daughter to me, I will teach her the violin, and you can learn the piano. I daren't suggest it however. I'd begun to learn the piano at a very early age from my sister Dot. I was five I think and Dot was ten and she was my teacher. Every lesson ended in tears. Finally Mom got tired of the upset, and said Dot was too young to teach, and I was too young to learn, so we gave up. I learned the violin when I was nine but gave that up too when I had to do homework at Grammar School.

We formed a family orchestra when we were all grown up, and married, and all the husbands were taught too, except my Eric. He didn't like the sound of violins. When I was learning I'd make weird noises. All the grandchildren also were taught. Two of them never played a funny note. We had three cellos, three violas and about fourteen fiddles. A cousin played with us and she hadn't got a good ear for keeping in tune but she tried very hard, and it all merged in all right when Mom and Dad and Dot and Julie and Ruth were playing, all very good. Kath and I were the least accomplished; our children did better than us.

A family Christmas Party in the 1950's.
Back row – Dot Eyles, Robert Sutcliffe, Hilda Baldwin and
Isobel Sutcliffe.
Front row – Dad, Mom and Marjorie.

One Christmas Dad had an ulcer on his eye and had a pad of cotton wool over it. We were playing the entry of the Queen of Sheba. I told Kath to get on Dad's blind side and just play the first note in the bar. It went so fast neither Kath nor I could have kept up, but crafty me, we got away with it. Dad's granddaughter Julie had pulled him through he said. She swelled with pride. He knew we'd all finished together and was delighted that we'd managed it. We always played at our Christmas party. When the grandchildren were too young to play in the orchestra Eric looked after them. We used two houses usually, one for the meal and for the children to play in, and one for the orchestra. We kept this up until 1965.

My four sisters and I went round the 65 clubs, entertaining. We sang part songs. A bit too highbrow I thought at first. We got lots of bookings, and did 26 engagements in a year. We went 18 years and really enjoyed it. We looked on it as voluntary work. These clubs were spread over a large area, Bradford, Halifax, Noristhorpe and Huddersfield. We didn't charge expenses as they were all struggling to keep going, looking after elderly people.

We had five different uniforms. Dot made us one set, which were the nicest I thought. We bought the others with great difficulty, as four of us were about the same size but Kath was plump and took a larger size. Once we had bought five identical dresses, buying a larger size than I needed, then Dot cut it up and added a bit on to Kath's to make it a bit wider for Kath. The dresses were a nightmare. They had metal buttons all down the front, which popped off when we sat down. The metal was sharp and cut through the cotton, which we used to stitch them back on. We carried safety pins just in case.

The day we bought them I was suffering from vertigo. It was quite a bad attack and they practically had to carry me across Bradford. They propped me up in the corner of the fitting room, and waited until they were sure which dresses we'd buy before I tried one on.

The Sutcliffe Sisters – Nora, Kath, Marj (standing), Dot and Isobel (seated).

We were never ever ill when we had an engagement. It kept us all fit and well. We practised new songs and rehearsed every Sunday after church, until midnight usually, learning new songs and harmonies for the engagements the following weeks. We averaged out at one a fortnight, although sometimes we'd have two in a week. When we completed a new programme a man from church made a recording of us. We were called The Sutcliffe Sisters and our opening number was 'Sisters' that the Beverley Sisters sang. We had 18 very happy years singing together.

When our church choir gave the Messiah, we had a lot of helpers, bringing the choir up to a hundred I think. Isobel Baillie came to sing the soprano solos. My Mom came into the choir, and the five of us of course were there as usual. We thought the headlines in the local press would be Isobel Baillie but instead it said, "Seven of one family sing in choir". Dad was choirmaster.

When I was in my teens Dad gave me a one-string fiddle. It had an ebony fingerboard and a silver metal horn with the round amplification speaker, similar to the ones on an old gramophone, and the two shaped pieces, to fit my knees a bit like a cello. I had to slide my fingers up and down the string to play the different notes. I could play any tune I knew with just a little practice. I was asked to play at a concert at chapel. Quite a highbrow affair. Derek Garside played his trumpet. When he grew up he became very well known. There was our best soprano, who later gave Nora and me singing lessons, and an elocutionist who went on and on, such a long piece I don't know however she remembered it all. Then it was my turn with my one stringed fiddle. I sat down with it placed firmly between my knees and then wondered if the front row of the audience would be seeing my panties. I pulled the horn down into position and all the children thought I'd broken the thing and laughed.

It was a bad start. My left hand could shake, and it was ok it put a little vibrato on to the note. My right hand though wielding the cello bow was also dithering. The smooth bowing I did at home had completely deserted me. This shaky bow was making the most dreadful sounding notes. People were wiping their eyes crying, with laughter of course. I stopped and told them I could play much better at home. They just kept laughing at every little thing I said.

When I'd finished they gave me an ovation and I had to give an encore. I was standing in the wings wondering if I should, then I decided it would be alright. I'd show them I could play. I went back on, and it was no better. I wished I'd never come back. The wavery notes sounded like a dying cow. Eric was sitting at the very back of the hall with an elderly friend who said, "She hasn't got a nerve has she?" Eric knew I'd terrified myself. I hardly spoke going home. Eric said, "Well you were the only one to get an encore". I felt I'd been a disgrace. I put the instrument in the front room. Next day I was listening to the wireless in the kitchen and I could hear a one stringed fiddle being played accompanying something, and it was even worse than I'd been. I dashed into the room to tell Eric to come listen. It was Eric playing. He cheered me up. I never played it again.

Marjorie plays one stringed fiddle in the back street.

I would like to try to play another one now. On the Internet there is one for sale for £300. Unfortunately after trying a ¾ sized cello, which was still too big for my hands, and wasting £400 on that, I don't feel like spending £300 on a one stringed fiddle. So now I have bought a recorder and we'll see if I can do anything with that! When you get old your idea of money price these days is all to pot. I still think a pound is quite a lot, and actually it's only like my Friday penny used to be.

Clifton Village had owned a set of handbells. The girlfriends and wives of the team members embroidered a lovely cloth of fine pure wool, embroidered in gold thread, with their name "Clifton Handbell Ringers". When Clifton Parish Council was disbanded and became part of Brighouse the bells were handed over to the leader of the Parish Council for safekeeping. The team had disbanded and no one else wanted to play them. The set of bells, about 200, were stored in Lister's Wire Mill for safekeeping. Mary Lister was my friend at that time and her father gave me a lift home every day with Mary, as we lived across the road. I always knew about those bells and who they belonged to, but they had been stored for years and years, and flooded twice and I imagined they would be ruined.

One day, many years later, the wife of the vicar of Hartshead wrote a book about

Clifton-cum-Hartshead, and mentioned a set of handbells which Clifton used to own. She wondered if anyone knew where they were. A man called Peter Fawcett eventually found them, they were in a terrible state, and got a team together. The team were mostly children and within a few months it was in danger of folding up.

As a last resort Peter came round Clifton in 1976 asking if anyone would like to learn to ring handbells. As a result my brother-in-law and Nora, Isobel, Kath and I all went to the house where the team rehearsed. They rehearsed in the back bedroom of this empty house. My sister Isobel didn't enjoy it and only went the one time. She felt it was too stressful. The rest of us loved it, and have enjoyed playing ever since. Many thanks to Peter for doing the research and finding the bells, giving us 30 years of pleasure.

Members of Clifton Handbell Team, playing at the wedding of two of its members, Paul and Margaret Marshall. Nora is next to groom, Kath and Marj next to bride and Clifford Riley behind Kath.

In 1986 we formed a team for retired people who could rehearse during one afternoon and I got Eric to join. He still rings every week and he is now 92 years old. I am now 86 and I think we are so very fortunate to be able to ring every Wednesday. It takes me longer to learn new pieces and I miss the odd notes or play a wrong note occasionally, but it is an achievement to learn new parts at my age. At first I was upset about my deteriorating skills, but the team wouldn't hear of my retiring, so I have to accept it and just do the best I can. 'Practice makes perfect'. It's a wonderful hobby and certainly keeps my brain alert. It's the most precise timing of all forms of music. Ten people have to sound like one person playing. Clifford my brother-in-law is 84 and is our leader. The rest of the team are all spring chickens. A lovely group of ringers, very special friends.

CHAPTER 8

Chapel

Park Chapel

Every Sunday from the age of three I went to Sunday School at Park Chapel in Brighouse. Dot took me, and we went to Grandma's for dinner, then back to Sunday school in the afternoon. This was for a year or so, until I was big enough to walk the mile uphill, back to Clifton and home, twice in a day. We had to take our dresses off at Grandma's and lay them on the bed, and play in our petticoats. We had a pack of cards with pictures on and we said "Snap" if two came up identical. We had to say "snap" quietly. It was Sunday. We had to be lifted onto the dresser top to have our knees washed, as well as hands and faces. Grandma was very fussy.

At Sunday school we learned little songs, which I can still recall, and we also played in the sand room. This small room had lino on the floor and a large sand tray took up most of the area. There were buckets and spoons and spades to shovel the sand, and small chairs around. One of my friends, also called Marjorie, had golden coloured hair, and she liked to play at having her hair washed in the sand. She put her head over the tray and I had to pour a bucket full of sand over her head. She must have kept her eyes tightly closed. She never complained of getting sand in them. We met up many years later and she talked of this happy time, washing her hair with sand. Her Mom wasn't very pleased seemingly, when she went home covered with sand. The colour matched her hair. We sang:

Whether the weather be fine

Or whether the weather be not,

Whether the weather be cold or

Whether the weather be hot.

We'll weather the weather,

Whatever the weather,

Whether we like it or not.

Smile, smile, smile.

It's well worthwhile.

For when you smile, another smiles,

And smiles come quick in piles and piles,

And soon there are miles and miles of smiles,

And life's worthwhile if you smile, smile, smile.

Once I saw a little bird going hop, hop, hop,

And I cried "oh little bird will you stop, stop, stop."

I was going to the window to say "How do you do,"

When he shook his little tail and then away he flew.

I remember the very first concert I was in at Sunday school. It would be prize giving probably. I had to be a cat. The costume was very small, and seemingly I was the only child to fit the outfit. I had to say meow and fight with a little boy dressed as a dog. I think I hadn't yet begun going to the Primary. A teacher came to our house to ask if I could be in the concert, and I remember hiding behind a chair, and wouldn't come out to talk to this lady. I was lifted on to the stage at the beginning of the concert, and told to fight the dog and the curtain was pulled back to show the scene. After a few minutes we had to run off and the rest of the concert took place. Then for the finale I had to sit next to the dog, with all the children standing round, and sing the final song. A man had to pull a sledge across the stage and he accidentally pulled it right over my foot. Well it hurt, so I cried, very loudly. Very, very loudly, and I upset all the children. You couldn't hear them singing I was making such a big noise crying. They gave me a small Christmas tree, which was decorating the stage, to stop my howls. I ruined the finale.

On another occasion when I was very young I was taking part in a concert at Sunday school and Dot my eldest sister had the main part. A large lady dressed as a gypsy had to hit Dot with her tambourine. She actually caught Dot's elbow with the wooden frame. Dot was supposed to cry, and she did. It hurt. The audience thought she was a wonderful actress.

Not happy memories. But all the other memories of Primary and Sunday school are happy memories. Learning the songs, playing in the sand room and lighting candles when I had a birthday.

Really the chapel provided the only social life we had, as well as our spiritual education and all our concerts, teas and supper parties took place at Sunday school. We knew everybody and everyone knew us. It was home from home.

Occasionally something would be too expensive for all of us children to go to, so none of us went in that case. Once they did a mock wedding and all the people at church were the guests. My Mum was the bride and she was dressed so lovely with veil, flowers and a long white dress, but we didn't go to the affair, any of us. Dad didn't like it anyway. He said they made it too real. The Bridegroom was Willie Smith who was very good looking! His young daughter was there and she asked Mum if she would be going home to live with them! Everyone who went enjoyed the wedding breakfast and all the funny speeches. The whole afternoon and evening made a lot of money for church funds as gifts brought for the couple were to be auctioned.

We had to make money all the time at Park Church, but it kept us busy and happy. It was a large church holding 750 people in the church itself. There was a big Sunday school room with spacious young ladies and men's classrooms, a Primary classroom, sand room and lots of smaller classrooms. The biggest schoolroom could be separated by forms into separate classes.

We had a large choir and a lovely organ. Dad was Choirmaster first, followed by Dot and they kept a very high standard of musicianship. We learned all the oratorios and gave Handel's 'Messiah' every Christmas. Guest singers came occasionally, well known people like Ida Bluer, Isobel Baillie, Scott Joint etc... They were people who sang on the wireless. These concerts were wonderful occasions.

When we had tea and a concert the 'Blaze Away Three', played music throughout the teatime. The three elderly gentlemen were Mr Riley on cello, Mr Wood on piano and Dad (Mr Sutcliffe) on violin. Their opening number was 'Blaze Away March' and that's where they got their name. At that time posh cafes had little groups of musicians playing for afternoon tea. It felt like that with the 'Blaze Away Three'!

When it was Whitsuntide we processed through Brighouse before a banner giving the name of our chapel. Two men carried this round, and we went to sing for people who were ill or very old. We then walked to a field and had a small currant teacake and a beaker of coffee. It always tasted good. We ran races, and our parents had races too. My Mom often won the Mothers' race. She was a good runner. Once she had a loose tooth which needed pulling out and Dad chased her all round the terrace. She didn't let him pull it, although her sister used to walk over a mile to our house when she needed a tooth pulling out.

Mom was once the heroine in the married ladies' concert, supposedly a young girl. As her hair was going grey at the temples we decided to give her a perm, and a golden rinse. The home perm was quite a success, but the golden rinse was a fiasco. Many tears were shed. With having a new perm, it made the hair very porous, and the golden rinse was many times more golden than ever we imagined it would be. A whole day was spent washing and drying and washing again this carroty coloured hair, using Lanry [4] and Persil and anything we could think would get rid of the golden rinse. It was the dress rehearsal that evening and Mom went in trepidation. However under the strong stage lights her hair just looked a natural golden blonde, and people remarked how young Mrs Sutcliffe looked. No one would ever think she was a mother to five grown-up daughters. It was quite a success.

On Saturday and Sunday nights the young teenagers, and older single people, walked around Brighouse looking for a new boy or girl friend. I never felt interested, and when I was 16 or 17 one Saturday night I had to go sing with the choir at a Saturday night lecture, given on the occasion of the Trust anniversary at our chapel. The lecture followed a nice tea, but was usually very boring. The choir sang perhaps two glees to add a little musical entertainment. When the evening ended there was just

---

[4] Bleach

time to run to a sweet shop at the other side of Brighouse, called Mr Who Are You's. Mars Bars were two for 3d, or 2d each. I arranged with my friend Nora to dash to this shop and we could each save 1/2d and buy our Mars Bar. We ran back to church, and people were still congregating and talking in groups as we arrived back. My Auntie Lottie appeared just as we reached the chapel, and with a horrified look on her face she said "Marjorie, I never want to see anyone belonging to me, walking around Brighouse on a Saturday night". I don't think she understood at all.

The lecture had been about pulpits, and modern designs for pulpits. Our pulpit was all carved and really beautiful. These pictures were to me very ugly. Like a barrel cut in two, and I think I said something to that effect. The American folks were looking for pulpits to put in their churches, and we were selling lovely carved ones, which I thought was a mistake.

Sunday School concerts were always enjoyable and by the time I was 15 or 16 I took part in an operetta. A girl had got tonsillitis 2 weeks before opening night and I was asked to step in. The operetta was called 'Aero Girl' and I thoroughly enjoyed it. I learned all the tunes and the dances, but not all the words, so sang my own, saying rhubarb, rhubarb where I hadn't learnt the words. We hired the costumes and the scenery and there was a full orchestra to accompany us. One night we gave six performances I think. During a ballet scene the girl behind me gave me a push, as she wasn't going to reach the spot where she should be. I fell, but jumped up immediately. A very plump lady afterwards said to me she'd never seen a fairy go down and get up so quickly and she wondered how she would have done!

Marjorie third from left, in a church concert.

The following year we gave 'Wildflower' and that was the last operetta. The cost to hire the scenery, librettos and costumes had increased and fire regulations cut down on the seating in our large schoolroom, so we couldn't make it pay. The married ladies still did concerts, which were quite hilarious. Later I joined this group and enjoyed taking part in many shows.

At Christmas time we had a party organised by the Snowdrop Band. This was an organisation in the church for women and girls only. It was inaugurated during the First World War and designed to keep young ladies chaste, faithful and pure. The snowdrop flower was the organisation's emblem. It met at least three times a year. There were one or two ordinary meetings, but the first main meeting was in November to give out the snowdrop bulbs and it was called Potting Night. At this meeting, after singing hymns, everyone bought three snowdrop bulbs, which they then planted in their gardens at home.

The second main event was the Christmas Party and then in late January/February we had Blossom Night. The snowdrops everyone had planted in their gardens, had to be dug up and taken along in a pot, where the lady who had grown the best snowdrops was awarded a prize. A former member provided the prizes for the best snowdrop. The group had a committee who were responsible for taking out the Sunday flowers every week to the sick and elderly and for visiting them at Christmas.

There was junior Snowdrop Band too for young girls and Father Christmas came along to their party. I was on the committee and took part every year in the charade, which we made up and acted for the entertainment at Christmas. The audience never ever guessed the word we were acting I don't think they ever tried. They just cried with laughing. We had a lady, Mrs Nellie Smith, who was a marvellous comedian and she only needed to walk onto the stage and everyone began laughing. It was always a success.

The Snowdrop Band disbanded when the Methodist churches in Brighouse amalgamated, although recently a small group have started up a Snowdrop Band meeting in one member's house.

Socials were very enjoyable too and the choir sometimes had dances and we sang glees. The men also had efforts to raise money and would give a concert and pie supper, we were always having to think up ways for making money. The boiler needed renewing, the whole church needed rewiring, and big jobs like these continually needed extra funds. Although the chapel was often full for special days like the anniversary of the Sunday school as time went on numbers began to drop and fewer members meant less collection on Sundays. Even more efforts were needed for fund raising.

Eventually we amalgamated with two other churches and our chapel closed down. It became an indoor market and later, when that closed, a public house! They have kept certain parts as features. The organ case and choir stall are still there. When I go in for a meal I sit and face the other way. I don't like to look at my seat in the choir, it breaks my heart. I don't go for a meal very often. As I got older I sat in church twice every Sunday and never missed Choir practice with Dad being the Choirmaster and after him, Dot.

CHAPTER 9

Clothes Hats and Weddings

Auntie Lottie, Dad's sister, made all our coats and dresses when we were young. She had pattern books with pictures of little girls modelling the coats and I used to choose one that had nice curly hair and a pretty face. I didn't look at the coat.

Auntie Lottie used to say, "Two frills on a dress for a small girl, then three frills when you grow taller." We had to walk over to the door in their living room and turn round slowly to see if the hem was level. Auntie was as good as a tailoress and she did the most beautiful embroidery on dresses of pure Woods' silk. This was from a silk mill in Brighouse called Wood's Mill.

We didn't have pockets on the outside of our coats. Sometimes they were double breasted with a belt or half belt, and two or three buttons on the sleeve. They were made from the finest Huddersfield cloth, which never wore, shabby.

Auntie Cissy was Dad's other sister and she bought the material for our dresses and coats, while her sister made them. We were not told that Auntie Cissy paid for the material until we were grown up. Auntie Cissy died very young, in her 40's I think. I think she had Glaucoma. She was a very kind Auntie.

We all had new dresses for Whit Sunday, with gloves, shoes and hat and a new coat for the September Sunday School Anniversary. When we were all ready for going out in our new finery Dad lined us up and said, "Now stand up straight, think on!" Once he shouted it through the open door when we'd already set off. Luckily the road was empty and nobody heard except us. We certainly knew it was no good having new clothes if you didn't stand up straight in them.

I loved to see Mom put the Sunday hats away on Mondays. When I was in bed ill, she came up to the bedroom wearing many hats, all piled on top of each other. They were put into hatboxes, which we kept under the beds.

We had hats at Whitsuntide. I had a lovely straw hat with pale blue chiffon pleated under the brim. And a little bunch of flowers on. The next door's cat was looking for a place to have her kittens and pushed the cardboard lid off the hatbox and climbed in. I found her, and put her

outside, but my hat was ruined. I had only worn it once.
I was twelve.

Sunday clothes were never worn, other than Sundays,
and Sunday dresses were taken off after morning Sunday
school and put back on after dinner, taken off again
before tea and hung up carefully.

We handed clothes down of course if we grew out
of them. Nothing wore out. They were made from the
best material you could buy. Auntie Lottie made them
always, and she was very good. As we grew older we
wanted them to be more stylish and Mom made them
for us. But all our childhood years Auntie Lottie did all
our clothes.

Dot my eldest sister then learnt how to dress make.
She bought very expensive patterns from Vogue – five
shillings – and once sent to Paris for a "faille", which
was a pattern made in muslin, not the usual paper. The
idea was to make it fit exactly, then unpick it and cut out
the material, and nothing would be wasted. It would fit
and be the correct length. One pattern was very nice
on Dot and Mom used the pattern for me and it was a
disaster, much too old for me. It looked very elegant on
Dot, but she was 20 years old and I was 15. The material
was also a disappointment. I had won 10 shillings in a
competition in the local paper where you had to make as
many words as you could from a long word, Manchester

I think it was, and decided to buy a dress length in the Saturday market. I wanted navy blue with a white dot, and Mom persuaded me to get a floral material. I never liked it. Years later when I got married I told Eric, my husband, about this dress and he bought me a navy blue with a white spot, and I loved it. I wore it with a straw navy blue hat, which was turned up at the front and down at the back.

When I was 15 my Dad's eldest sister got married. We thought she was quite old to be getting married but I don't suppose she was really. Kath and I were bridesmaids. We had pink and blue dresses that had a panel of lace frills in the centre skirt, and a cape collar of lace frills. We wore velvet scull caps with blue forget me knots round, white lace gloves and posies of flowers made at the Co-op. The stems were inside the cone, which came to a point. It was too long I thought. We held them, having our picture taken, and decided our hands looked like a duck's foot. The photo was taken out in our back street. Aunt didn't want to go for the usual photographs. When she was buying the dress she asked for something suitable for a garden party. This auntie was the one who made our new clothes.

Kath and Marj as bridesmaids.

When Kath and I were at Grammar School we had two Christmas parties on the Saturday. Juniors were in the afternoon and seniors followed immediately. Kath was going to the early party and I was going to the senior one. We went to a shoe shop in Brighouse for a pair of silver shoes to fit both of us. The man was in our choir at church. He came with two pairs of shoes. We said one pair to fit both of us. He found some too. Kath handed them to me as I came in to school. We timed it just right. Everyone was looking at a girl who was being taken home in a cab, with a beautiful black horse in front. They had a taxi business, but the cab made us think she was a princess in a carriage.

That year I had a pale yellow crepe dress; Mom cut it out on the floor and the material moved. The front panel was shorter than the rest of it. Dot persuaded me that it was better, short at the front, better for walking in. She could always make me feel everything was for the best.

Mr Hurst, who lived two doors below, was a bank manager. Their front room was papered in panels. I thought it was so beautiful. They had two grown-up daughters and three grandchildren. We used to play with the grandchildren when they came to visit. Once I had a bottle of nail varnish, and was doing everyone's nails, but the grandchildren dared not let me do theirs without first asking their Moma. She said so long as I didn't put any under the nails, it would be alright. Our Mom didn't ever fuss about such things.

We often got dressed up and gave a concert in the back street. Once we made a cover from a parasol into a skirt for Nora. I once had a lovely fairy frock, white with silver tinsel ribbon, which Mrs Oldfield gave us. Once she supplied me with a real Robin Hood costume when I went to night school and we had a rag day.

Mr Oldfield had a leather shop in Brighouse. Everyone mended their shoes, their weekday shoes maybe, and had the cobbler to do their Sunday ones. Dad had so much practice he became as expert as the cobbler himself. I wanted ankle strap shoes, but never had any. Mom wanted us to have support across the instep always. I had very narrow feet and was difficult to fit with shoes. Kath had plump feet and had no trouble at all.

Our heads were small also, so hats were more expensive when they were a small fitting. Most hats were still made too large for me. Mom said I'd expensive feet and an expensive head too. I got a craze for hats when I was in my teens. I saved my spending money up, and bought a hat. They were about 4s 11d, four shillings and eleven pence, and one lovely navy blue felt was 2s and 6d in the sale. It was my favourite for quite a while and eventually someone stole it when I put it on the floor at my feet in the Ritz cinema. I had had my money's worth from it, but still went back on the Monday to see if the cleaner had found it.

Another of my favourite hats also got lost. I lent it to my sister Dot. It was a grey pillbox type hat, and my mother-in-law had given me a piece of fur to stitch round it. Dot went in an open car, and put the hat on her lap. When she got out, it rolled away without her thinking about it. She lived up a steep hill. Someone at the bottom of the hill found it and took it to the Armytage Arms public house and put it on a window bottom, thinking someone would claim it. It didn't make me happy hearing all this. Obviously they thought a type of lady wearing this grey pillbox hat with grey fur would be a frequenter of the Armytage Arms public house. No one claimed it so it was given to the cleaner, who gave it to her daughter. I never got it back and somehow I didn't want it anymore.

Once there was a coal strike, around 1939/40. We got quite without coal, but Eric had some blocks of wood, which he promised to bring round as quickly as he could. Mom was frightened that if she let the fire go out she would never start it again so she kept our fire burning by using some of my collection of hats. She knew if it went out nothing would light big blocks of wood. My hats saved the day.

Our next door neighbour was a dressmaker in her spare time, and once made a blue velvet bonnet with a white ermine trim. She came round to try it on Isobel, our baby sister who was about one-and-a-half years old at that time. Isobel thought the bonnet was being made for her and ended in tears eventually. When the lady tried it on, Isobel said "Suits her, fits her" and smiled, very satisfied with herself. It was being made for another child, and actually I thought Isobel suited it far more than the little girl for whom it was intended. I thought no one was as pretty as Isobel.

I remember having a dark blue coat made for me by my cousin Vera. It had a white fleck in it and I bought extra material to have a hat made to match. A milliner had a hat shop in Brighouse and made hats herself to order. Somehow the hat didn't suit me as well as the one she had made for my cousin. Vera had passed all her City and Guilds' examinations and although she never went to Grammar School she ended up teaching in five schools around Plymouth. She died at 33 years on a bus taking her to work. It was a kind of pneumonia, which was going around at that time.

The hat and coat I kept for Sundays. One day I came home from work and Mom was obviously upset because she'd given my hat and coat away. It was at the time of the Spanish war, and a refugee had come to Clifton bringing nothing with her, she just had the clothes she stood up in. The councillor lady who brought her to see Mom knew she had five girls, and it happened that my size fitted, so Mom gave it away. She explained how dreadful it was for the girl to have left her family and everything behind. I didn't mind by the time Mom finished, in fact I felt glad to help, and the hat didn't do a thing for me anyway.

When an elderly aunt got married we weren't bridesmaids but had new apple green dresses and felt bonnet hats to match. The dresses had puff sleeves with a high yolk. Kath and I were always dressed alike for special occasion. We liked it when people thought we were twins. These apple green felt hats were too babyish I thought. A neighbour came to inspect us before we set out for the wedding and said it all suited Kath, but it's criminal to put Marjorie in green. I have never worn green until I retired, and then decided to take no notice. Green is a lovely colour. Blue suits me much better though.

When I started work at 16 years occasionally I could buy silk material for making a dress. If a customer went bankrupt and owed the firm I worked for, for the silk, we some times received material instead of money. I had one or two striped silk dresses, which Mom made. The other office girl also made herself a dress, and we looked to be wearing a uniform. Some silk went to make parachutes, and parachute chord, during the war. This chord was very very strong although only as thick as my little finger. It once pulled a lorry, a heavy lorry, which needed to be pulled onto a road. It was amazing, the driver had laughed when it was offered for him to try, but it succeeded. I made underwear from parachute silk. It never wore out.

When I got married I wanted six bridesmaids and a long white dress and veil. Of course we didn't have enough coupons to do all this, and Dot persuaded me it was so much better to have a nice dress that I could wear afterwards on Sundays. She said you don't want it to look like a concert. As it turned out we were married at 8 o'clock on a very foggy Saturday morning. None of the photos came out apart from one, and even on this one Eric was hidden in shadows and I only had half my face showing, because of my large black hat. That photo has all faded away now. The one train taking us to Conway left Brighouse station at 9.28. We had to eat the wedding breakfast (it was haddock), go up home for me to get changed, then back to the station for 9.28.

It took all day to get to Conway. I had had my tonsils removed just two weeks before, and not had any solid food for ten days. I usually weighed 6 st 4 lbs but I had lost 12 lbs. It took Eric's Mom six weeks to get me back to my 6 st 4 lbs. I then donned my wedding clothes and had a photo taken in the lovely garden, which was to be our first home.

CHAPTER 10

Pets and Rations

Once we had a lovely tame dove given. It sat on my head. It was just before Christmas and we had decorated our front room with paper festoons. I wanted my Dad to see the bird sitting on my head. He was due home, and I must have sat perfectly still for about half an hour. Just as Dad walked in at the back door the bird did its droppings all on me. I shewed it off, and it flew on to first one and then another of those paper chains and brought every one of them down. We had a cycle shed in the back garden, and thought the dove could sleep in there. We put in food and water for it and it seemed quite happy. Later in the evening our Nora went to look at it, and as soon as she opened the door it flew away. We went looking for it but never found it.

The top house of our terrace had a parrot. It pulled the feathers out of its tail. We wondered if it was unhappy. It bit through its wooden perch. They made a new one out of a buffet leg and it was biting through that too, so they covered the ends with an oxo box, which was made of tin. The nephew used to visit and always came to our house to play. He was a very nice looking little boy. He said he'd marry me, because I always knew what to play at. He became a doctor eventually, and quite forgot he'd planned to marry me. His auntie came to live near me and my husband Eric at the end of her life. We lent her a bedside table, for as long as she needed it. Eventually she went into a hospital and died. Geoffrey her nephew had to dispose of her things and we never got our table back. He wouldn't have known it was on loan.

Once a farmer's dog found some little hedgehogs, and he gave my friend Polly and me five little ones. We fed them with milk and bread and put them in Polly's coal cellar. We thought they'd be secure there, and we'd take them to school next day. By morning they had disappeared. We couldn't imagine how they got away, but they did. We were very sad about that.

I remember the first frog I caught. I had taken Isobel my youngest sister for a walk in her pram, and we had gone along a lovely country lane when I noticed a movement in the grass and found this lovely frog. I had it in my hands but didn't know how to keep it. I quickly took Isobel's sock off and popped the frog in the sock and carried it back home swinging from the pram handle. On reaching home we found an old washing-up bowl and put water in it and the frog, and a stone for it to sit on. I put it under the privet hedge and dug up a little worm for it to eat if it was hungry. I thought it would be perfectly happy to live in our back garden. But it had gone before morning.

Kath loved tortoises and had a big, old one for many years, called Tommy. We told her it might feel lonely on its own so Kath bought one called Ziff, which was short for "As if we haven't enough without it". As soon as Ziff came Tommy died. Kath didn't think it was dead and after we'd buried it she still dug it up in case it was asleep.

Isobel loved animals and she often carried the Co-op cat home for lunch, and took it back after dinner. The Co-op was just near Clifton school. She loved dogs too, and went to be a kennel maid and took the dogs out on long leads. We couldn't have a dog at home because we hadn't room. It wasn't until three or four of us had got married and left home, that Mom said Isobel could have a dog,

Dad went to Bradford market with strict instructions to buy a male dog that wouldn't grow very big. We called him Raq and had him for at least a year before Isobel, our youngest sister, said she thought Raq was a girl dog. We did wonder if we should change her name to Rachael, but never did. She grew to be as big as a young donkey, but she was a lovely dog.

Mom and Raq on the front steps of 139 Clifton Common in 1941. Look at the neatly ruddled and whitened steps!

When Raq fell ill, Mom thought it was canker in her ear, and brother-in-law Ray took her to the vet to be put down. That day I had got a chicken for dinner and had done all the trimmings, and then sat down alone and cried. Eric was in India, and I couldn't eat this special treat, so I took it to Mom's. She gave it to the dog for its last meal and Ray then took it to the vet, who said he could easily cure Raq's ear. They came back home with the dog's tail up in the air. The chicken had really done it good. There was no pet food to be had and they had to survive on bread with marmite. It was very hard for pets too during the war.

Because Isobel was the youngest, Mom let her join the Girl Guides, the only one that did! Mom thought it was a military tendency and never let us join. We were able to put her right in time for Isobel to join. Mom was a staunch Labour supporter and we used to help at election time taking numbers. It was always exciting at Clifton as it was always a near thing. The Conservatives had a car, Labour people had to walk. Once a car full of Conservatives broke down and couldn't reach the polling station before 9pm. It had four people aboard, and the result was changed because Labour got in by just three or four votes, after recounts. When Mom died the Labour Party sent a wreath of red roses. Dad would never tell who he voted for. I wondered if he was a Liberal.

When I think of the time, working as cashier bookkeeper, I remember the director's dog. It was a very old wire-haired terrier called Peter. It sat in front of my small electric fire and kept all the heat off me. I tried to move it by walking past so that it had to move, but it just settled down again right in front of the fire. It also made smells. It was a very old dog. The mill yard ended at the towpath of the canal. A six-foot wall dropped down onto the path. Once a horse, which was pulling a heavy barge, came along, nodding its head, which was on the level of the mill yard. Peter the dog went berserk barking at the nodding head and frightened the horse, which fell into the canal. The bargee was very cross. The warehouse men and the mill manager and foreman all came to help to get the horse out of the canal. They managed it with a struggle. Peter wasn't popular that day.

During the war we really learned how to manage on very little. I always took the top off the milk every evening and shook it up in an empty treacle tin. It made 2 small pats of butter, enough for my breakfast. My sister had some evacuees, a mother and her two very young boys. Dot looked after them and her own two girls. 4 children under 4 years. We lent Dot our box mattress to make a bed on the floor for her two girls, and the two boys and the mother had Dot's children's beds. The lady came from Hull and was very nice. She had always lived with her own mother, as her husband was in the forces. She herself had never cooked or baked. Dot took over from the mother. Years later Dot sent Christmas presents to the boys and lost count of time. She sent toy guns and they were now 6 feet tall.

In 1940 we had quite a lot of air-raid warnings and used to sit on our cellar steps and down in the cellar. I once slept down all night, as the all clear didn't waken me. The rest of the family, apart from Dot's husband Max, all went back to bed. Max and I were both asleep with our heads under thick stone slabs. We decided if the house was bombed we'd rather be killed than injured and thought these shelves would certainly finish us off.

Mom always wore her corsets if there was an air raid. She put them on over her nightie to hold her together. She also had Mrs Oldfield to look after. Mrs Oldfield came round as soon as the sirens started. We all sang in the cellar as loud as we could to drown the sound of the planes. Mom would say, "I heard them, you've no need to be singing", but it passed the time. We used to say "That's one of ours" and then guns would go off. There was no kidding Mom. Dad of course stayed upstairs in bed. He said there would be more deaths from pneumonia, than from Germans bombing Clifton. We sat with our gas masks on our knees and a clothes peg in our mouths, all wrapped up in eiderdowns and thick tab rugs on the cellar floor.

From left to right – Isobel, Kath, Nora Dot and Marj c 1946. When this photo was taken the sisters were on a day trip to Huddersfield with a 'show' in the evening. Nora was sitting on a table and just before the picture was taken she fell off! They were all laughing so much that the picture was nearly impossible and they had no handkerchiefs with them, having left them in their bags in the waiting room.

CHAPTER 11

Further Education and Work

After I left school I went to a newly opened commercial college in Brighouse for 1 year as my parents wanted me to continue my education as long as possible. After that I went to night school for a six-week course to learn the newly introduced 'Pay as you Earn' tax scheme. It was compulsory I think in those days. I did a course of business studies and was the only girl in the class. The rest of the students were all boys and they worked for all the large companies in Brighouse. The job was considered to be a man's job and many of them had come along with someone else. I was on my own and had no one to discuss things with. Any thing I didn't understand I put my hand up to ask to be told again until I did know. No other person ever said they didn't follow any specific bit, but I didn't worry anyway; I knew it was important that I understood, as I had no one to ask at work.

Some of the lectures were about supply and demand and I didn't agree with the principal at all. The teacher said that if there was a demand then the price must go up. I thought it got cheaper making large quantities and so the price should go down. The teacher insisted I was wrong no matter how I argued. He worked during the day as a private secretary for a firm. Forty years later Eric and I bought his lovely bungalow. I don't think he remembered having had me in his class arguing with him! Eight more people had wanted the bungalow, but luckily we got it and it was delightful.

I once got 10/10 for my homework and these boys were put out. One of them grabbed the sheet of my homework, threw it on the floor and stamped on it, leaving a big dirty shoe pattern all over it. This boy was always immaculate with Brillcream on his hair, which was brushed straight back. I got my hand at the back of his head and pushed his hair all over his face, then pulled his tie round to under his ear. He thumped me. The teacher of course was not there; he'd gone home quickly that night. I cried and this horrid boy walked me home all up the steep hill to Clifton. I didn't speak to him at all. He was sorry though and apologised. He ended up a director of a company, but died quite young.

After the course finished and the P.A.Y.E. started, the firms with two or more cashiers who had been on my course kept ringing me about points they had not understood. I smiled to myself. They had not wanted to look small in front of the class by admitting they hadn't followed some of the lesson. I had had no such worries!

It was all straight forward and simple really once we got into it.

The aquarium was perhaps the means of my getting my first job. Every open day at school I had to go to the lab and stand by the aquarium ready to explain and answer any questions. The chairman of the governors always came up to the laboratory and had a look at my aquarium. He used to tell me he had caught 'bull's heads', a type of toad tadpole. The job I got first was at his firm! He owned a silk mill and needed a new cashier/ book keeper/ wages clerk, and I got the job. My friend Catherine Tart also tried for it and as her parents played bridge with one of the directors she thought she would be certain to get the job. We were both just as clever as each other, but the director didn't want her to pay his salary in case she told her parents how much he was paid! Being friends was a handicap not an asset!

At the mill I had my own office. It had all the books in a large safe. I had to do these books, also the wages. I was cashier and bookkeeper, quite a daunting job. These ledgers all looked alike. I was terrified of making a mistake. The wages were very complicated. The women were all on piece. Some machines were modern, and went faster. Some were slower and a living wage could not be earned, so a graph had to be used and every 1lb of yarn, all at different prices, had to be calculated. I carried a box round to all the different departments. It held little lead pots with a brass number 1-80. I had to learn everyone's number. When I was being shown the way, down cellars, into the engine room, warehouses and spinning and warping sheds etc, there was a small sliding door, which was narrower than the box. I was warned always to be very careful going through with the box lifted slightly. I was careful, but then just once I knocked the box against the side of the opening. My heart sank. I quickly opened the box to look and there was no money between the pots. I thought thank goodness, and continued on my round, paying the wages. I hadn't gone far when they found their wages were incorrect. They all had a good idea how much they'd have earned. Some got more, some less. The silver and copper had jumped out of one pot into another. I had to take it all back and do them all again.

One day, when I had been doing the job for a while I was walking home from work with Dad. He worked in the next mill and I liked to wait for him to walk home. On this day he asked me what wage Emily Colbeck would get? I said, "Oh Dad, I haven't to tell, it's all very confidential."

"Good girl," Dad said, "I know if you won't tell me, you'll not tell anyone." He was very proud of me. I loved my Dad and always thought he was the very best Dad in all the world.

When I went to work there I found a pistol in my drawer. I don't like guns of any description, being a pacifist, and got the director to throw it into the canal. He had gone on a safari to Africa and had the gun there. I couldn't work with a gun in the drawer. I was taken to the bank every Friday morning to collect the money to pay the wages. The chauffeur John Walls drove quickly over a little bridge to make my stomach jump. I called him every week. Towards the end of my working days at the silk mill, petrol became very scarce and I had to walk to the bank. It was quite obvious I was carrying a wages bag, and we paid a small insurance for cash in transit. I said "Oh is that in case I get nobbled and hurt" and they said "No it's for if the money is stolen, we're not bothered about you". Well I was most put out and said "if anyone looks at me as if they are going to steal the cash, I shall give it to them". I think they enjoyed pulling my leg.

When I started work as cashier and bookkeeper I got 15 shillings a week. The auditors came and checked everything and I hadn't done anything wrong and the chief auditor told the directors that they weren't paying me enough. They always raised the wage each year by 2 shillings and 6 pence, but they gave me a five-shilling rise. I worked there eleven years and got £3-10sh finally. By this time we were at war and I was married.

I'd known Eric for a long time. He, Clifford and Robert were all friends and went around in the same gang. They told him he should ask me to go out with him and so he decided to do it. When Eric rang me to ask if I would like to go to the theatre with him I was at work, in the 'top' office. I answered the phone and was surprised to be asked to go to the theatre with Eric Shooter. I covered the mouthpiece and told Eleanor, the office girl, what Eric had said. She said, 'say no!' so I uncovered the mouthpiece and said, 'yes alright', just to be contrary I suppose. And now we are on our 65th year of marriage. I am glad I was contrary!

My husband was manager of a department of a large firm and he had a very good wage, I think £5 a week paid monthly. The day before he went into the army we bought his parents' house for £700. Eric went next day to Richmond barracks, and I removed into our new house. We had been living in rented accommodation across the road. A man with a horse and cart had been booked to move everything. Thirteen of my relatives came to give me a hand, with Eric having just left me for the army. Kath took a basin into the back garden, as the raspberries were all ready for gathering. She spent all afternoon gathering them, and then ate them. She was on leave from the A.T.S.

When Eric joined the army I got £1-8-0 a week. I had to pay the mortgage £3-6-4 per month. I earned £2 a week by then so had to save every week to pay the £3-6-4. It was almost one week's income, but I managed it. It only cost me 12 shillings a week for food. I didn't buy a newspaper or a bottle of pop. I couldn't think of any other things to cut down on. I once walked to work across the valley to Southowram, then walked round that village collecting insurance, eating my sandwich for dinner as I went between the farms, but came home on the bus after tea. I remember getting home and just lying on the rug with my coat on, too tired to take it off until I'd had a rest. I did that job for twelve months.

Isobel wasn't happy working at a laboratory and Eric was due to come home from India, so I let Isobel have my job and I went to work with Kath at the Pru. Isobel was too young to have the Pru job. We both moved and got 10 shillings a week less wage, but Isobel was happy. Why I had to do it for a year was the army kept putting Eric's demob back. He came back in April 1947, all safe and sound.

When I left they gave me a very nice reference for the Prudential manager. I never took a copy, so never had a reference.

When I became Registrar for births, deaths and marriages and the previous Registrar who had trained me left, I asked her to give me a reference, as I'd never kept the one I'd had, and she said I didn't need one. To have been a Registrar was looked on as the top job for clerical work. I still wanted her to give me one, which she did. Of course I never used it. I was sixty-two when I retired from being Registrar. How I loved that job. I would have done it for no salary if the council had said they couldn't afford to pay me. I enjoyed it so much.

In my first job I never needed shorthand, which was good as I wasn't good at it! Typing wasn't necessary as I only had to type statements every month and the other office girl was a shorthand typist and very good indeed. I had to be good at maths for reckoning up the wages, which really were complicated. They had to be correct of course; in fact I had to be a perfectionist the whole time. It was very good training for me especially when I got the job of Registrar at a later date. That really does have to be faultless because it is important to keep the legal records perfectly. There are ways to correct everything, but it's much easier to not make any errors in the first place.

Being the Registrar at Brighouse was much quieter than at Halifax. I always had plenty of time to take doing the register, so could take every care. If there was an error it took such a long time sending documents up to London and waiting for instructions about sending evidence etc... far better to be very careful in the first place. It's a man's job really and you are paid equal pay if you are female. Doing this job I worked variable hours so I wasn't classed as part time. Of course undertakers could come to the house at any time outside office hours. Once one came in the hearse with the coffin, and parked outside our bungalow. It was soon after we had moved in and it caused great concern to the neighbours!

CHAPTER 12

Illness

When I was about two years old the doctor came to see Grandad who got bronchitis every winter. He'd worked down the mines as a young man. The doctor had a big head and short legs and wore half spectacles at the end of his nose. He looked like a gnome. He took an interest in all of us. He sat in the kitchen after seeing Grandad and talked to Mom. We had a small stool, which was for me. We always called it Marj's buffet. The doctor was going to sit on it and bent right down, but just as he was on top of the stool I ran round and whipped it away and he fell on the floor with his legs in the air. My Mom was mortified. I was too young to know I shouldn't have done it.

My only serious illness seems to have been the rheumatism in my legs and knees, which kept me in bed for a long time. It started when I was 6 years old and I got pains in my legs. People told Mom I'd got growing pains, but Mom thought there was no such thing and decided to call the doctor. I had to stay in bed for seven weeks. He said that complete rest would prevent me having rheumatic fever. If my dinner was a bit late I remember feeling at my flat tummy and thinking I was starving to death. This, mind you, if it was ten past twelve instead of twelve o clock!

At the end of seven weeks it was Christmas and I did get more presents that Year; one was a very big pot doll with a mass of dark curly hair. Two years later Nora broke it. She fell while crossing the road with another little girl. The bus was coming and Nora's friend Ada picked her up, but the bus ran over my dolly. I was very upset and Mom pointed out that it would have been far worse if Nora had been run over. As she had already broken two baby dolls that wore long nightdresses, but had no hair, by banging their heads together, Kath and I thought she must be going through a clumsy stage and we were still very upset.

That Christmas at the end of my illness it was decided we should all go to Grandma's in a cab. Kath said, "Isn't it lovely when our Marj is poorly and we can have a ride in a cab!" However the expected black cab and horse didn't arrive, a shiny new big car came and took us instead. The firm had changed over and funerals etc... now had a hearse.

The last funeral that had the black horses and cabs was about this time. If Mom knew a funeral would be passing our house she drew the curtains as a mark of respect. I was in the front room when she did this and she told me not to be peeping under the curtain. As soon as Mom went into the kitchen I went under the curtain and saw the funeral pass. The black horses had a black plume on their heads. Mom came and caught me and smacked my leg!

I was at Cromer when Isobel got scarlet fever. When people in the village got this disease they had to go into isolation because it was a serious disease and could leave the patient with complications. The houses had to be stoved and the family had to stay away for several hours. Isobel was taken in the fever ambulance to Clifton Isolation hospital. She was nearly five years old. Mom and Dad said they felt dreadful, like refugees, not being allowed back home for so many hours and being told to keep away from friends and relatives in case they spread the infection. All the cupboards and drawers had to be left open to get the fumigation everywhere. When the letter arrived at Cromer telling me that Isobel had scarlet fever Mrs Greenwood held the notepaper with coal tongues in case of infection and she burnt the letter after we'd read it. I don't suppose the stoving did any good, only to quieten people's fears of the germs spreading.

There was an outbreak of smallpox when I was eight or nine maybe. A large family who lived in Kiln Fold at the top of our terrace had got this frightening disease. I had been playing with the youngest member of the family. Not all of them got it, but it caused quite a panic. Mom gave us all a large spoonful of "yellow jam". This was something she made which moved our bowels. It was sulphur and treacle, and kept in a large stone jar. We all had a good clean out, and presumably any germs were got rid of. We didn't get smallpox. The house we retired to 26 years ago belonged to the family that had had the smallpox all those years before.

I always liked to watch men work, although not the window cleaner. I was in bed for quite a long illness, seven weeks, when the window cleaner came. I shot under the bedclothes and stayed there until he had finished. He called out to me to say I could come out now, he'd finished. He was a jolly man. I met him many years later and didn't recognise him. He reminded me how I wouldn't look at him at work. I was the Registrar by then, and he had a different hairstyle, and looked very genteel and elderly. His hair was white and long. He looked altogether different.

The dentist also came to Clifton school and brought his chair and set it all up in a little room just off the baby class. It was very upsetting hearing some crying and others yelling and one boy even ran away and the dentist ran after him into the playground.

We never had our teeth attended to at school, but took each other to Mr Murgatroyd, the dentist at

Brighouse. Usually he worked on his own, but once had another dentist working with him who had a very heavy hand. Dot took Isobel and Isobel bit the dentist's thumb because he was pressing too hard on her face. He was furious and refused to treat her, and Dot called her all the way home. He later became a school dentist.

If a first tooth became loose Dad pulled it out for us. He got a hankie, put it over his hand and said, "Let me just feel if it is loose enough to fall out." Then he took it out. My Mom wouldn't let Dad pull her teeth, but her sister always came to have hers out. Dad had a very good firm grip and could pull double teeth as well. He pulled peoples teeth at work if they wanted one out, no cocaine or anything.

Some people fastened strong thread to their loose tooth and fastened the other end to the oven doorknob with the door open. Then they walked away and got someone to close the oven door. Then the tooth would come out.

I remember the time Mom had all her teeth taken out. They looked quite good teeth, but I think the problem was her gums. When she came back home from the dentist we had her saying tongue twisters. I am sure she'd not have felt like it, but she played with us and made us laugh, trying to say Sister Suzie's sewing shirts for soldiers. Mom made sure our teeth were checked regularly and we all kept our own teeth, always.

None of us ever had a corn or bunion. Great care was taken when buying new shoes to see they were a good fit. How I longed for ankle straps but never got any. Mom put Vaseline on the Sunday patent leather shoes, to try and prevent them from cracking.

When I was about seven years we played doctors and nurses and once I ripped my arm on a rusty nail. They didn't bring me home as we were playing at hospitals, so they wrapped it up saying how wonderful to have real blood to deal with. The scar is still there. It is about an inch and a half long and has white dots on it. A scar I had on my knee has now disappeared. It was always there when I was a child.

The doctor used to come every year or two to school, to check on us. Our chests were sounded and throats examined, tonsils checked and teeth inspected. It was a lady doctor, and every time she looked at Kath's and my tonsils she said she didn't know what to say. They were enlarged, but not diseased. We used to tremble in case she advised Mom to let us have them removed but she never did.

We were also weighed and measured. When I went to Grammar School I stepped on the scale following a very big girl. It made me look very light, as they had to take off all these weights and move the arm on the bar of the weighing machine. I was a pound for every inch, 52 ½ inches tall and 52 ½ lbs in weight.

Dot used to dislocate her shoulder quite often. If she used a tennis racket, which was heavy, her shoulder dislocated. Once it came out with carrying Isobel to bed when she was big enough to walk. Dot couldn't get it back and the doctor came and gave her an anaesthetic on the rug in the front room, and put it back in. I remember coming home that evening and Mom coming in to the kitchen with a finger to her lips, to tell us to be quiet. Kath and I could smell the anaesthetic and that day Dad had got his head cut at work. A metal bar had hit him, and we thought it was to do with that. We had to sit quiet in the kitchen until the doctor left and we learned then it was Dot's shoulder. Dot worked for Dr Smith and he had come from Mirfield to make her better.

We were never conscious of being squashed in our little house. Everyone talked at once, but we were all able to follow every conversation around us at the same time we ourselves were talking. The authorities came round and said we were ½ overcrowded. We owned our house and we did talk about removing, but Grandad fell and broke his hip. He had always said he wouldn't move and we had to leave him his bed and a chair and table and he would stay at Clifton – that decided things! Our next door neighbour had become a widow and she was nervous being alone at night, so they arranged one of us would go round every night and sleep in her back bedroom. If she became ill we had to go fetch my Mom immediately, though she never was ill.

I was the one who had to sleep next door. It was a colder house than ours because she let her fire go down, waiting for me to come from the commercial college. I was always cold. Sleeping by myself was also much colder, but I had to do it for a year or two and then Kath was asked to do her turn. Mrs Oldfield made our breakfast Sunday morning as a thank you treat. It was very nice too. She whisked up an egg and added breadcrumbs, pepper, salt and butter and fried it in the pan that bacon had been cooked in. It was tasty. I never made it quite as good for myself later.

At home we had two double beds in the front bedroom, and we slept two to a bed. No one wanted me because I curled up and they slept straight out. They said I was like a snake. I used to make up stories to entertain them, silly stories to make them laugh. We'd smuggle sweets to bed for a midnight feast, but it would be about 8:30 really. Being able to make up stories came in very handy many years later when I had my son.

Once when Eric, my husband, had flu and we sent for the doctor, our son, who would be six or so, said to his Dad, "What would you be doing if you weren't in bed poorly?" and Eric said he'd be digging up the brussel sprouts in the allotment. Andrew said, "Right, I'll do it" feeling he was now man of the house.

Within a short time he was back saying the fork had gone through his toe. I was taking off his Wellingtons and had him sitting up on a kitchen table washing his foot and saying, "Oh no, it hasn't gone through your toe!"

He said, "It has, I had to pull it out."

I looked under his toe and sure enough there was a hole. With manured ground, it was important to have tetanus jabs. When the doctor came four hours later I had been making up stories all that time to keep Andrew happy. Being so full of the accident I almost showed the doctor out after he'd seen to Andrew and said we'd to go to hospital. I had forgotten Eric upstairs with the flu! But the doctor remembered, fortunately. Our kind neighbour took us to Halifax hospital and insisted on waiting to bring us home. He waited five hours. We always had lovely neighbours wherever we lived.

We had a hut on the allotment and Andrew once cooked two chips in fat, in a typewriter ribbon tin, for his friend who was later home at teatime. Andrew left his briefcase with all his books, he went to the commercial college that I first attended, and he popped back home for some reason. The fat was being heated over a candle and of course it all got on fire, the whole hut burned down! All the neighbours were alarmed, not knowing if any children were inside. The allotments were over the wall from our home, very handy.

CHAPTER 13

Briggus', Clifton and further afield!

At Clifton they had a Faffen Fuffen Band in the old days, which was revived again. A Faffen Fuffen Band is made up of people blowing tommy talkers, combs covered in tissue paper and any other instrument possible. Everyone dressed up in funny costumes, like country yokels, which is perhaps why Brighouse people often joked about Clifton Village, making out we were a bit simple! The story went, that once a farmer put his pig on the wall to watch the Faff and Fuffen parade! and this tradition was still kept when the band was revived. A pig was scrubbed very clean and went round on a lorry in memory of the first pig. My sisters and I went in the parade dressed like country gawbies; everyone else had hired fantastic costumes! We blew tommy talkers and went all round the village making as much noise as possible.

Faffen Fuffen parade 1977. Marjorie in white jumper and silly hat next to Kath and Nora, Ray Snell in front of them.

During the festivities Clifton Handbell Ringers played their music in a tent and on one occasion Morris men came too I think. Two men, Trevor and Douglas, led the procession playing piano accordions and a lovely atmosphere prevailed making it feel like an old village again.

Robin Hood has a very strong connection with Clifton and is, in fact, buried in Kirklees Park. I quite believe this and gave a talk about it, at Grammar School, when I was only twelve. In Robin's day England was covered by forests, which reached down to Nottingham and beyond. His wicked Prioress cousin, who bled him to death, lived at Kirklees Priory and I think he lived near Wakefield so would know all this area. Robin was my hero. He was so good to the poor people of his day.

I don't know how he could find the strength to shoot his last arrow, to be buried at the spot where it landed. Those bows would take a lot of strength to pull, but he managed it.

When the Technical School I attended had a Rag Day I went as Robin Hood. One of the helpers there, took some of the money we raised at the event, he was a con man. Afterwards I was on the Clifton bus going home to change and saw this man who had been helping to count the money from the collecting boxes. He had caught my bus to Leeds. Later the police came to Baldwin Armitages, where I worked, and asked to speak to Robin Hood. I had to describe the man and he was caught in Leeds. Apparently he went round helping to count money at galas and fetes and managed to steal some each time. He got caught this time!

My Mom told us about Hal, a sort of jester, who entertained at Kirklees Hall. A joiner who worked there tormented Hal, who was mentally backward. Hal waited his opportunity and when the joiner was having a nap he cut his head off and hid it under the shavings in the workshop saying it would be a surprise when he wakes up and can't find his head. It was a while before Hal realised what he'd done and he never got over it. He died very unhappily knowing what he'd done.

We had a brass band at Clifton who rehearsed in a band room. One joke was that one-day someone came and said it sounded lovely out there, so they all put down their instruments and went out to listen!

Saturday night I loved to go into Brighouse and look around the market. It was an outdoor market with lots of interesting characters selling their wares. I learned the prices of everything, and got very agitated if a person agreed to buy something, which hadn't quite reached its bottom price. Hanging NAPHTHA lamps illuminated the stalls and straw was spread for the stallholder to stand on sometimes. A man came with a snake draped round his shoulders. He sold ointment, which contained venom, to cure rheumatism – "Always rub from the side to the centre" he said. Then there was a very clean immaculate man selling medicine. Doctor somebody. A Jewish gentleman sold haberdashery, on the floor. He didn't have a stall even. After a few years he had a stall and sold material. He ended up with a very nice car, and a very nice quiet wife helping him. When he was on the tarpaulin on the floor he sold elastic, and used to say, "You can boil it, stew it, fry it, you can do everything with it".

The man selling lino unrolled it and hit it very hard each time he brought down the price. There were sweet stalls and pot stalls – one lady wished to buy a chamber pot and noticed he kept the money in it, so asked "How much is the till?" – veg stalls and fruit stalls, stalls full of knives and second hand clothes stalls, and food – roast chestnuts, roast potatoes and ice cream. All very interesting, and it closed about nine o'clock.

It was dark in winter, and the gas lamps cast shadows. My shadow was before me, then behind me, as the light dimmed halfway to the next lamp. There were dark corners and bends in the road at the bottom of the hill. I always felt a little nervous until the road straightened, and sometimes I would go to the drapers' shop where my cousin worked, and wait to walk up home with her. The shops closed at nine on Saturdays. Shop work was very tiring. Long hours standing behind a counter, not allowed to sit down if there were no customers. Very often I bought a cream puff to eat going home. Six pence!

The shops in Brighouse were all very friendly. One Christmas, we were having the family party and needed a new Father Christmas outfit. Eric was always Father Christmas. I went to a men's outfitters and explained I needed a red dressing gown for our Christmas party. The manager said, "Oh don't buy one I have just the thing at home. I'll bring it down and you can borrow it." Where else would that happen I wonder?

Another shop, a dress material shop, was always very kind to my eldest sister. She chose some material, which was cut off the roll, then Dot, realised she hadn't brought her purse. The shop girl said, "You'll need your bus fare to get home, I'll let you have it. I'll keep the material or you can take it and pay later if you wish."

In Clifton everyone knew everyone else. There was a Post Office, which sold sweets, two other little sweet shops, and a third one, which was part of a house going down the hill into Brighouse. One of these shops was owned by a friend whose three daughters were friends of me and my sisters. They sold ice cream, and if there was any left when the delivery man came to take back the empty tub, Mrs Tattersall put it into a basin and brought it down for us to eat. It was kept cool with ice round the tub. No one had fridges in those days of course.

The lamplighter came round every day to light the gas lamp, which was at the back of our house. I learned how to climb it and we also fastened a rope and swing round it. That wasn't the best of ideas as we ended up getting a bump. It was nice watching the lamplighter. He was a very tall, slim man. He didn't bring a ladder unless it was to change the mantle, or the timer in later years; he brought a pole with a hook, which he used to light the gas. Later they made them light automatically.

We used to have concerts in our back street. It wasn't a street of course, it was just the back of the terrace of houses – a rough road, wide enough for the horses and carts that came round selling pots and pans, and other fruit and veg, and the coal man, and the cart that I never saw, which came to empty the toilet.

Mom and Dad with Julie and baby John Snell showing the back street.

The toilet emptying cart always came during the night. Once it came in the morning and I was very small, and was using the toilet and heard all the noise of a shovel. Seemingly I finished and went back and Mom, realising what was happening, said, "What did you do when you heard the man?" and I said, "I finished". We used to cut newspaper into squares and thread a piece of string through to hang up behind the door. Some people with large families had two holes and even three, but we only had one. Just one house in Clifton had a water closet. It was a "tumbler" and worked from the kitchen sink. We thought it must be very dangerous; it was very deep.

Our bath was made of zinc and hung on a hook down the cellar. It was to carry up every Friday and put in front of the fire. I had to be first because I had long hair, which took a lot of drying, and then the others went youngest first. The water was heated by the fire, and the other side was the oven, which baked everything. Later we got a gas water heater, which was very good, we always had plenty of hot water. It was always warm and the towels all heated to wrap round us. Much, much nicer than the very cold tiled bathroom, pale green bath and wash basin, which I had to use when I left home to marry Eric. This new bathroom in the new semi was the pride and joy of Eric's Dad. I really longed for the warm kitchen fire and the zinc bath, although emptying it had its problems. If you got tired of ladling it out down the sink and risked lifting it up when there was still quite a depth of water, it came over the top and wet the rug. It was a stone floor, so nothing to spoil.

Another man that came round was selling yeast and he carried a small weigh scale. Everyone needed fresh yeast to bake bread, and that is all he sold. His name was Mr Nobbs, and he was related to the Clifton Mr Nobbs who owned a donkey. That Mr Nobbs had a coffin under his bed for many years before he died.

We got skipping ropes made from plaited straw from the man who sold vegetables from a horse and cart. He was known as Peggy Martin, though Mom said we had to say Mr Martin. These lengths of plaited yellow straw were used to fasten barrels of apples etc. A man also came round carrying a big suitcase with elastic and ribbons and tea towels and dusters etc. I can't think he'd earn much, and it must have been a heavy case to carry.

Another man came regularly selling nettles. We called him the nettle man. He had a curved spine. He came when the nettles were young and fresh and we always bought some. Mom used them as a vegetable, sometimes with young Pash docks – I suppose "passion" would be the name. It would be Easter time I suppose.

Everything wasn't wrapped up when bought like it is now, bread, for instance. Ladies had a shopping basket with a serviette to cover things up. Sugar, currants and raisons were bagged, butter was patted and some shops stamped a pattern on it. Not the Co-op though, they just made it square and wrapped it in greaseproof paper.

No one had a fridge in Clifton, but all seemed to have good keeping cellars with stone shelves. Food was bought when in season and no one ate pork when there wasn't an R in the month. During May, June, July and August we ate beef and lamb. We had chicken at Christmas every year. It was a gift from a man who knew Grandad. Seemingly Grandad taught the man a lesson and he was very grateful and showed his gratitude by always bringing us a lovely big chicken for our Christmas dinner. Some people would not have reacted in the same way because Grandad had been quite shocking really. This man had brought a handful of money from his pocket to show Grandad how well off he was. Grandad jerked his hand making the money roll down a grate, and said, "Never do that again". He was quite a character.

On another occasion when he was gardening a man walked by that he knew and Grandad asked if he would like some rhubarb. The man said, "I am not particular", meaning yes please. Grandad didn't give him any. The man waited and eventually said, "Aren't you going to give me some rhubarb?" Grandad said, "Well you said you weren't particular and I am not particular either." He never gave him any!

People grew vegetables in their gardens and fruit bushes too if they had room. After I was married we had a large garden and also two allotments. We grew all our own fruit and vegetables. My husband enjoyed gardening in the evening and at weekends. It was a nice change from being office manager. Our son grew up knowing the names of all the plants in the garden. Other boys his age knew the names of makes of cars. Our son was more interested in birds, the feathered variety!

We always went blackberry picking every year. There were loads of bushes. They only had fruit for a short number of years, and then nothing. It happened all the time. We'd go to where it had been a good harvest, and the bush would be bare, but one that had been poor would be laden the following year.

Only one man had electricity. He had a generator in his cellar. Electricity did not come to Clifton until after the war. Many had paraffin lamps. We had gaslights with mantles, which had to be changed if they became damaged. The gaslight was lit when it was coming dark and it stayed lit until the last person went to bed. It was pulled on by a chain, the central light. Wall lights had a tap to turn. One was in the staircase to light the landing, two in the bedrooms, one in the kitchen and one in the room. It was quite a good light and a soft glow in the bedrooms. Once when my sister Dot was small she found the pile of new mantles in a cupboard and put one on each of her fingers. She was just playing with them and a hole came in each mantle.

Shopping for the neighbours and for Mom was always a pleasure. We had to say "No thank you" if offered a penny. The Co-op smelled so nice in those days. Everything was weighed out and wrapped up in blue bags, and everything smelt so appetising somehow. Sometimes the manager would give us a sweet. Big boys carried huge 'pokes' of flour on their heads. Sometimes I'd take my dolls' pram and wheel the shopping back home. We only had one dolls' pram, they took up too much room. Our toy box was on the floor just inside the back door. Children all knew where to look for things. Once we changed it and made the bottom of a cupboard beside the fireplace into the toy box. Mom was ironing, and a little boy whom she'd never seen before walked into our kitchen and crept under the ironing board and went into the cupboard toy box to find something, then quickly ran back under the ironing board and out of the kitchen. A friend of Mom's was sitting on a chair chatting to Mom while she ironed, and asked who that one was. Mom laughed and said he was a stranger, she'd not seen him before, but one of us must have sent him because he knew just where to go.

The houses in Clifton stand on land owned by Kirklees and the householders had to pay ground rent to Kirklees up to a few years ago. Another company bought the leasehold from them and people were given the chance to buy the lease for a few hundred pounds according to the area of land taken up by the house. When the leases were set up the law made it plain that the price of the lease was set up for all time. Ours cost us £1.20 a year. To help the company my Eric has always collected all the neighbours' money and sent a cheque saving them all postal order poundage and stamps and helping the company as they send every receipt to us to distribute to the neighbours. The amount is so small that it can't be a worthwhile project until the houses fall down. The land is very valuable, but no good as long as houses are built on it. I can't think it will stop the sale of a property to hear that you must pay £1.20 a year for the land!

We didn't do our own decorating when I was a child, we had it done professionally and it lasted quite a few years. The painters were two brothers, and they did an excellent job. It took them three weeks to paint the outside. They spent over a week preparing it. It was brown paint, varnished and grained, and it lasted years and years. The inside of the house was papered and the kitchen had a varnished paper which was quite pretty at first but it later "went off" and looked faded.

What a time the lads had stripping that paper many years later! They all helped each other, and later when one brother-in-law removed and needed decorating all through his quite large house, complete with varnish paper in the dining room, they ended up using Clifford's acetylene burner to get it off. The lady next door happened to be Clifford's auntie and she came round to say the butter was melting on her pantry shelf. She said, "You must have had a big fire yesterday". The house was cold and had been empty for a while so she thought we were warming it up.

At holiday time occasionally Mom and Dad took us to a park where there was a boating pool. If we all took just one friend each it meant there were ten children and Mom and Dad, but there was a very big rowing boat and we all fitted in. Dad rowed. It was a heavy boatload, and eventually he stopped for a rest. A frantic little voice said, "Watch your work Dad". This was because I thought Dad's rowing was what kept us afloat. "Watch your work Dad" became a family saying. We certainly enjoyed the holiday trips to parks in other towns. One attendant for the boats was Grandad's brother. We often went to Shibden Park to see Uncle Randolf at his post, looking after the boats. Another of Grandad's brothers was Uncle Fred. He could make the noise of a cock crowing very lifelike. Grandad was the nicest looking one I thought. He had rosy cheeks and white hair and a long white beard. He always wore a tail jacket. Mom had to cut his nails for him and they were very hard and brittle. Grandad was a Communist I think. He did not doff his cap when Princess Louise passed by in a taxi. All the other men held their hats in the air, Grandad stood with his hands in his pockets. We had a photograph of him. We felt ashamed of him really, although secretly I thought he must have been brave too.

Royal visit to Clifton, July 1912. Irvine Baldwin is in the far left of the photo with his cap on his head and his hands in his pocket. He is standing in front of his home in Forrester's Terrace.

The first holiday I remember was at Southport, at Mrs Newton's. I remember the name because Dad sang a song "I am going to carry our Dorothy home, all the way to Mrs Newton's". Dot wasn't a good walker, and I had to get out of the pram for Dot to have a ride. Her ankles were weak. They bought her a pair of blue kid boots, which cost £5. This was before I was born. Years later if Dot wanted something we'd say, "But you had blue kid boots". Things would have been expensive in the First World War and Dot was born in 1914. Dad carried us all on his shoulders. I loved being high up, holding his hat, feeling perfectly safe.

The second time we went to Southport was when my son was five years old. We went with my sister Kath and brother-in-law Ray, and their little three-year-old daughter Julie. It was quite an exciting week really, although a bit horrendous for Julie. Firstly she fell in the boating pool. Her Dad fished her out as soon as she fell in, and fortunately they had brought a change of clothes for the first time. We had a long mile and half to walk back to the boarding house. The next thing happened two days later. We were at the zoo and a large monkey reached through the bar and the safety bar and grabbed Julie's hand. It would not let go. I was giving Ray my hatpin, fortunately he knew better than to antagonise it further. Ray eventually prised open its hand to release Julie. I asked her what it felt like to be holding hands with a monkey, and she squeezed my hand as hard as ever she could.

We had just calmed down and moved round to a cage with a very big rabbit. When we stopped to look, this large creature ran round and round its cage then stopped in front of Julie and squirted water, urine, all over her. Poor Julie, it was all too much for her. Their car broke down, and we had to ring Nora and Clifford to take them home. Eric and Andrew and I came back by train. It was one of the holidays we remember.

The lady who owned the boarding house had been hurt in a bus accident. She wasn't really fit to have visitors.

She left a feather duster in the bedroom so that we could dust. I wondered what the kitchen would be like. On the final day she asked me to go into the kitchen and it was absolutely spotless. She said it was all she could do. We didn't go ever again because of the long walk to the beach. The sea was out of sight when the tide was out. Miles and miles of golden sand of course.

Most of our holidays have been spent at Scarborough. I won't fly anywhere and Eric won't sail anywhere, so Scarborough it had to be. And now we enjoy staying at home. There's no place like home.

CHAPTER 14.

Loyalty, Christmas and Expanding Families!

Christmas was a lovely time when we were all young at home. We were very fortunate, especially when times were hard – 1928 I think was the general strike. Christmas time we always had a pillowcase each full of presents, and they came from Mum and Dad's friends and aunts and uncles. We had more than people with an 'only one' because five was such a lot and friends made sure we all had a wonderful pillowcase full.

At school the teacher of the infants' class cut out large brown paper stocking shapes, which we sewed. She then went to the Co-op which was just across from the school, and the kind manager saved up all the free samples, always enough for one for each child, and we filled the stockings. Holiday times we had to take a plant home and keep it watered, and I remember dropping this heavy pot which broke, and I left it all in the gutter and cried all the way home. Mom found a new pot and went back and potted it safely. It felt such a big calamity to break the school's plant pot. Mom always came to the rescue.

The Primary Christmas party was the highlight of the year. Father Christmas came with a sack on his back full of presents. The year that I was in bed for seven weeks before Christmas, my Auntie Lottie came upstairs to ask which I would prefer, a mirror and comb in a case or a manicure set. She said "I shall be Father Christmas this year at the Primary Party, so I can see you get your present, the one which you like best". I was quite shocked, as I hadn't realised the Ladies' Committee took it in turn to be Father Christmas. Then I remembered the previous year thinking Father Christmas was wearing ladies' shoes. Of course, as long as my youngest sister believed in Santa we had to go along with the story, and Isobel was quite old before she disbelieved.

In my youth, the winters seemed more severe, with snow falling. We wanted a sledge. Dad made us one from a baking board. He put wooden runners under it, and bored two holes for a piece of clothesline to hang onto and pull it back up the slope. It was almost square, and the other children shouted, "Make way for the table". Another boy used his mother's frying pan. He placed his cap in it then sat in it, holding the handle, as it turned round and round as it went down the hill.

Our sledge wasn't high enough from the ground, and the snow wet our knickers. It was very uncomfortable. The field where we sledged was very good as it rose up at the bottom to slow us down before hitting the wall. Sometimes we went down a cobbled hill, then through a farmyard and down a field. It was a long haul back, but a wonderful ride down. This farm, Mr Snowball's, was the one that supplied our milk, and lovely cream. Six-penny worth filled a very big jug. It was our Sunday tea treat. It also had a pear tree and we bought a cap full for one penny; usually 24 pears for a penny. Sometimes they were a little hard and woody, and not much flavour. I suppose we should have kept them a few days before eating them.

Mom made jam and marmalade and lemon cheese. She also put eggs into water glass to seal them. She bought extra eggs when they were cheap, and used them in winter when they were dear. We kept two bread crocks specially for the pickled eggs. We also made ginger wine for Christmas. It was very strong and burned your throat. We had it with Christmas cake and cheese. The wine glasses were very thin and on a delicate stem. We had to be almost grown up before being allowed to drink ginger wine from a wine glass.

Mom and Dad always thought the world of all their sons-in-law and the boys all treated them so well, like real sons. Of course three of the lads were firm friends before they married three of the sisters so that helped to make a strong bond. We all got on very well together. In fact we thought of all our brothers-in-law as brothers and they treated us all as sisters.

Parties at Christmas were always very special. We had all the old fashioned games like charades and forfeits. Matthew, Mark, Luke and John was a good one if you hadn't got a very comfortable chair to sit on! We prepared written puzzle games and special games for the little ones like Chinese lady and flying and then there was the orchestra. This was always wonderful and quite thrilling when we all played carols together with Dad conducting and all the stringed instrumentalists of many different standards. One year we even tried a version of the 'Queen of Sheba' for string orchestra! And we all loved to sing too.

A Christmas party in the late 1950's/early 1960's, with all the 'children'.
Back Row – Shirley, Julie, Andrew, John and Mavis.
Front Row – Jane, Ruth and Nancy.

CHAPTER 15

Funerals

I think I've been to more funerals than I can count, but to bring my story to a close I will describe the deaths of my Grandad and my parents.

Mom looked after Grandad for many years and as he got older he was more and more dependant on her. I could see Mom was getting very tired and her hair was going grey at the temples and she looked older. One day I said,

"Couldn't Grandad go to hospital?"

Mom said, "Maybe I will have to let him go."

She spoke to the doctor and he said it was too late, Grandad had only days to live. The night before he died, Mom got us all in the kitchen sitting around her knee. She said, "Grandad is going to die tonight, so when you get up in the morning and walk through the room, turn round and look at the piano. Don't look at Grandad's bed." I did this and never saw Grandad dead. Kath peeped and saw him, she admitted to me years later.

Because Grandad had died we were all farmed off to relatives until after the funeral. He was to be laid out in the front room during this time and we were not to see him. Death was treated very differently then, people were kept at home after they died, not sent to a chapel of rest. This could be quite difficult in a small house, having a large coffin on a trestle in the living room! Our cousins went to see him laid out, more than once, but my Mom didn't allow us to go home until it was all over. He was buried in Clifton Churchyard. We had never to take cut flowers; he wouldn't have wanted that, so we planted snowdrops on the grave. We thought of him in heaven with his very nice Eliza. I never knew Grandma Eliza of course, but had seen photos of her. She looked very, very old in a black beaded cape and hat. She was only in her fifties, but looked much older than her years in the long black dress and cape.

The shut up bed was given away and a sideboard put in its place.

On the 4th July 1965 Dad died. It was on a lovely, bright sunny morning and Dad was just saying they would get up and go for a walk up Highmoor Lane, as far as the second seat. He was laughing, as he often did, when his leg gave a sudden jerk and he died. It was a terrible shock for Mom. She rang for the doctor and got all of us and seemed to be coping very well, but got a pain in her chest as she told the doctor how Dad had died and had to lie down on the settee. By this time Kath, Nora and I were with her, Dot was still travelling over from Low Moor and Isobel not there yet either. Nora had been most involved in ringing everyone and giving the sad news of Dad's death. The doctor fetched a tablet from his car for Mom. This was a warning for us, but we little expected what was to happen.

Three days later Mom was all ready for Dad's funeral. She was looking at the many cards and letters, which arrived each day. When suddenly, at 8.30 am Mom collapsed on the floor and died, just four hours before Dad's funeral service. We were not able to let people know and had to carry on with the funeral service as planned.

Park Chapel was packed with people at least 700 people, some of them standing, and as the Reverend John Wren announced at the beginning of the service that the service was to be for Mr and Mrs Frank Sutcliffe, the whole congregation took in a breath together. It was a gasp of shock and it made a very loud noise coming from this large group of people. It was a most strange experience and the memory of it has stayed with me. Although we were all very shocked and very sad to lose both our parents together we felt that it was lovely for

Mom and Dad. They had been so happy together for over 50 years, always loving each other and making such a happy home for us, they couldn't be parted by death.

The doctor who examined Mom explained that our hearts don't break, they are just a bag of muscle, but when, as with Mom, a blood vessel breaks in the casing of the heart it is the nearest thing to a broken heart. We went to Mom's committal service later that week, on the Friday.

Mom and Dad at their Golden Wedding.

My niece Ruth, who was just a little girl at the time, asked me if any more would be dying. I said,

'No, we are all being looked after very carefully because we look after each other, and we always will."

CHAPTER 16

Final Thoughts

I think that music made all our lives so much happier. Now after 64 years I have finally retired from the choir, but still support them anyway I can. We have got a really wonderful church choir still and a marvellous organist. Central Methodist Church is well worth a visit if you are ever in Brighouse. You will find a warm welcome there.

Our family has always been special and kept close, mainly I suppose through Mom and Dad. They loved us very much and were delighted when we all got married and they then, at last, had five sons. They wanted a boy always, but when a friend offered to swap his son they said "Oh no!" They wouldn't swap one of us, which was very nice. I wrote a poem about our family once, five sisters, five husbands, eight children and Mom and Dad. Here it is:

We're just a small family, twenty in all,
We think 't'world of each other it's true,
When I was quite young I said, 'I love mysen',
As a matter of fact I still do.
But Dad says we're clannish, it happens ta' much,
For we all stick together like glue.
Yet breakin' one stick is quite easy yer' know,
But try ont' bundle yo' do.
We've nobbut one rule and it's no fallin' out,
For birds in their nests should agree,
If we didn't we know we'd have trouble 'bout doubt,
Dad'd 'ave a day's work givin' nineteen a clout!
To be sure of't right culprit yo' see.
We know we had't very best Mom in all't world,
And't most wonderful Dad, aye it's true.
No doubt you love yours just as much so I guess,
So to all't Moms and Dads then, 'Goodneet and God
bless'

A photograph which appeared in the Brighouse Echo at the time of Mom and Dad's Golden Wedding.
Back Row – Isobel, Marjorie, Dorothy, Kathleen and Nora.
Front Row – Dad and Mom

I am now the only sister left. I get very special treatment from my remaining 'brother' and my special nieces and nephews and of course I still have Eric, Andrew and Bronwen, his wife. I have ever been thankful and very grateful for my large family – we have such happy memories. Especially of Christmas.

Time seems to just fly and I can't believe a week has gone when it only seems like a few days. Maybe it's because I am slowing down and taking more time to do the jobs, with rests in between, which of course I never needed before.

Well to enjoy every day is wonderful, so I say, 'Thank you' and look forward to enjoying tomorrow. One day at a time is now our motto. One day at a time.

Eric, Marjorie, Bronwen and Andrew

ABOUT THE AUTHOR

Marjorie Sutcliffe, 27/07/1919, is a lady of spirit and true northern grit. Born into a musical, Methodist family, of Clifton, near Brighouse, West Yorkshire, she still lives there with enthusiasm and humour, making light of her own misfortunes and always looking for the good in everyone. Her story spans five generations of Yorkshire folk and is told with such charm and sincerity that one suddenly realises how the passions, hopes and fears of people long since gone can be just as warm and real now, as then; when brought to life by such a skilled storyteller. Her characters explore our common journey with dignity, purpose and compassion and are described by a lady who has obviously loved every minute.